Teach Yc

WORDPERFECT
Versions 5.0 and 5.1

Ann Elms and Fenella Deards
Kingston College of Further Education

Hodder & Stoughton
A MEMBER OF THE HODDER HEADLINE GROUP

ACKNOWLEDGEMENTS

Trademarks

MS-DOS is a registered trademark of Microsoft Corporation

WordPerfect is a registered tradement of the WordPerfect Corporation

A CIP catalogue record for this title is available from the British Library.

ISBN 0 340 54920 3

First published 1991
Reissued 1992
Impression number   15 14 13 12 11 10 9 8
Year   1998 1997 1996 1995 1994

Typeset by Focal Image Ltd.
Printed in Great Britain for Hodder & Stoughton Educational, a division of
Hodder Headline Plc, 338 Euston Road, London NW1 3BH by Cox & Wyman
Ltd., Reading, Berkshire.

TABLE OF CONTENTS

USING THE WORDPERFECT TEXT DISK

Many readers of *An Introduction to WordPerfect* will be experienced word processor users already and merely wish to cross-train onto Word-Perfect from another package. Experienced typists may also find that after the initial chapters they no longer require the keying in practice offered in the book. In both these cases using the accompanying text disk will be an advantage.

You will notice that we have used the same filenames for the exercises stored on this disk as used in the book, for example 'EX2C' is the third exercise provided in chapter 2.

If you have a twin floppy disk system follow this procedure to take a back-up copy of a text file, i.e. EX2C. Carry out the start-up procedure to obtain the A:\> prompt and then place the master text disk in drive A and a blank formatted disk in drive B. Key in 'copy EX2C.doc b:' and press ENTER. Your screen will indicate when copying has been successfully completed.

If you have a single floppy disk and hard disk system follow this procedure to take a back-up copy of a text file and store it on the hard disk. Carry out the start-up procedure to obtain the C:\> prompt and then place the master text disk in drive A (the floppy disk drive). Key in 'A:' and press ENTER. The A:\> prompt should now be displayed on your screen. Now key in 'copy EX2C.doc c:' and press ENTER. Your screen will indicate when the file has been copied.

We suggest that you only copy over those files from the master text disk that you are actually going to use. Be sure that once copied you only use the back-up version. If you use the master version you will not be able to repeat the exercise at a later date as it will have already been amended.

1 INTRODUCTION

1.1 About this book

Welcome to WordPerfect! WordPerfect is a powerful, easy-to-use word processing package with many sophisticated features which this book will introduce to you.

It gives instructions for using WordPerfect 5.0 and wherever necessary the authors have included instructions for WordPerfect 5.1, especially where this varies from version 5.0. Where different instructions are not given for the two versions, this means that the same procedures apply to both the versions. However, instructions are *not* given for using a mouse with WordPerfect 5.1.

One of the most obvious differences is in the wording of the questions WordPerfect displays on the screen in response to instructions given by the operator. For example, in Word Perfect 5.0, when F7 is pressed, the screen prompt is 'Save document (Y/N) Yes', whereas in 5.1, the prompt is 'Save document Yes/No', with 'Yes' highlighted.

It is worth mentioning here that WordPerfect always offers the user the safe **default**. A default is the instruction given to the computer which the program assumes the user will want to select. In this case, it is assumed that the user will want to save and so the word 'Yes' is highlighted and can be selected by simply pressing the ENTER key. Should the user not want to save, 'N' must be keyed in instead. This procedure prevents the user from inadvertently losing work by carelessly pressing the ENTER key. Note also that both upper case ('Y' and 'N') or lower case ('y' and 'n') are acceptable to WordPerfect.

This book is intended for the newcomer to word processing, those who are familiar with word processing but have never used Wordperfect and wish to 'cross train', those who have started to use WordPerfect but feel the need for some help with mastering the package and its more advanced features, and those who are new to using a personal computer. Look in the Glossary to check the meaning of computing terms, where you are unsure.

All the basic features of word processing in WordPerfect are covered, plus all the intermediate features and a high proportion of the more advanced ones.

However, not all the most powerful capabilities of WordPerfect are covered in this book, because the authors felt that by the time you had gained a certain proficiency in using the package, you would be able to look up features with particular relevance to your work in the manual, which is supplied with WordPerfect.

1.2 What is word processing?

Word processing is so widely used now that for many people life would seem strange without it. Once you have learned how to use a word processing package competently, you will never want to revert to typing or handwriting text again!

Using a word processor you can quickly and easily do the following:

- Alter the appearance of your text and the layout (called formatting), by using facilities like emboldening, underlining, italics, double-line spacing, etc
- Number pages automatically
- Set, alter and clear tabulation stops easily
- Control where the page of text breaks
- Alter margins
- Left or right alignment of text, centring, justification (making right margins even)
- Copy, move, and delete text
- Spell-check document
- Use the thesaurus
- Save, merge, rename, and delete documents
- Use headers and footers on long documents
- Use left, decimal, centred or right tab stops
- Use maths function
- Use print preview feature to see how your document will look when printed

- *Plus many more facilities.*

When word processing documents, the computer sends your output to the screen before it is printed. This enables you to make alterations and additions to it, before a paper printout (called hard copy) is obtained. Sentences, words and paragraphs can easily be re-arranged to give a more satisfactory end-result to your work.

The ability to communicate more effectively by presenting your work in a more attractive, readable form can lead to more creative writing and can be important for your business and personal life. Having said that, it is not a miracle answer to all problems, and it is necessary first to master the package, which is where this book should help you.

1.3 WordPerfect

WordPerfect is one of the most popular word processing packages available. Because it is such a powerful word processing program, it requires a relatively large amount of memory in the computer, so only machines with a big enough memory will be able to run it.

It has many advanced features, which are accessed through a series of menus. These menus are accessed through the function keys. Each function key from F1 to F10 has four possible uses when combined with the three special computer keys: control (CTRL), alternative (ALT) and SHIFT. A template which is supplied with WordPerfect, and can be placed above the function keys on the keyboard gives a summary of how these keys can be used, either alone or in combination with others.

You will find that when you access certain menus you will immediately be faced with another menu from which to choose an option. You have the choice here of either pressing a given number or the first letter of the option you require. In this book, the numbers are usually given, but it is equally acceptable to choose the first letter of the menu.

1.4 The keyboard

You will need to have an IBM-compatible computer system in order to be able to use the WordPerfect program. The computer will either have twin floppy disks or a fixed (hard) disk, with a single floppy disk drive.

There are two common keyboard layouts which are illustrated below. Other keyboard layouts are available, but these are the two you are most likely to encounter.

Figure 1.1 The standard keyboard

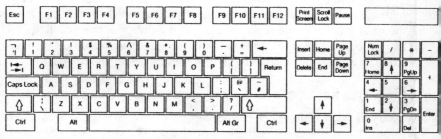

Figure 1.2 The standard keyboard

Use Figures 1.1 and 1.2 to locate the keys which you will be using for word processing.

ALT — alternative key used in conjunction with function and alphanumeric keys to carry out word processing instructions in WordPerfect

BACKSPACE DEL — deletes the character to the left of the cursor

CAPS LOCK — a toggle key which produces capital letters (or lower case if the SHIFT key is held down at the same time)

CTRL — control key used in conjunction with function keys to carry out word processing instructions in WordPerfect

DEL — deletes the character the cursor is under, or any blocked text

ENTER — starts a new line or instructs the computer to process a command you have given

Function Keys — WordPerfect relies heavily on the function keys to access the menu system and to carry out the main functions of the word processing program

INS — switches on the overtype mode when using WordPerfect

NUM LOCK — a toggle key which can be used to enable the numeric key pad on the left of the computer keyboard to be used, instead of or as well as the numbers in the top row of the keyboard

SCROLL LOCK — a toggle key which causes the UP and DOWN cursor keys to move the text on the screen a screenful at a time

SHIFT — produces the characters shown in the top half of the keys, such as the " mark above the number 2, or produces capital letters when pressed at the same time as a letter key. Also used in conjunction with function keys to carry out word processing instructions in WordPerfect

TAB   moves the cursor to particular points on the screen
                             (called tab stops). The computer will include pre-
                             set tab stops but these can be altered by the user.

Some of these keys are described as **toggle** keys: keys which are
pressed once to activate a particular function, and pressed again to
switch it off, i.e. CAPS LOCK.

Chapter 9 gives more information on the use of quick functions with
the function and cursor keys.

1.5 Presentation style

The book has been presented in a consistent style throughout and you
will find that text which you have to key in as a practice exercise is
typed in single quotes like 'this' or if there is a larger section of text
to be entered, then it is inset from the left margin of the book. All the
practice exercises conform to this procedure.

To illustrate the text and help you appreciate what to expect on screen,
illustrations called **screen dumps**, appear in nearly all the chapters. A
screen dump is shown below as an example of what to expect when
you first get into WordPerfect.

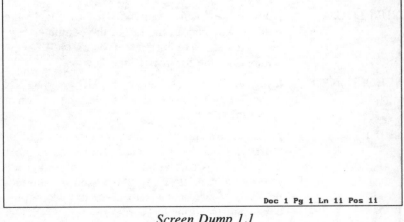

                                                Doc 1 Pg 1 Ln 1i Pos 1i

Screen Dump 1.1

Reference is made throughout the book to CTRL, ALT, and SHIFT, which often have to be held down whilst you press another key such as a function key or a letter key on the keyboard. The key command is always shown in capital letters, which also applies to the use of other command keys such as ENTER, BACKSPACE DELETE or TAB e.g. Hold down SHIFT and press F8 (to activate print menu).

Where new concepts or words are mentioned for the first time, they are printed in **bold** and usually have explanations of their meaning near them.

The layout of your text when you key it in has largely been left for you to decide and it should be possible for you to work with the **default** margins of WordPerfect, unless specific instructions are given to the contrary.

For standard text, it is current practice to block the text from the left margin and not to use an indented first line for a new paragraph. The left margin should normally be at least one inch to allow room for filing papers in a ring binder, and should be wider than the right margin.

1.6 How to study

If you are completely new to personal computers or to word processing, you will probably need to work through the book in the same order as the chapters are set out.

It is suggested you do not try to cover too much in one session, but ensure you have sufficient practice at one new concept, before moving on to the next. Work at your own pace, ensuring that you understand what you are doing, and that you have retained the actions you have to perform without having to refer constantly to the text book to see what to do next.

However, if you already know how to word process but do not know how to use WordPerfect, you will find that you can skip through the book quite quickly initially, looking up the features you want to use.

If you have already started using WordPerfect, just look up the features of interest to you. It is not necessary to work your way through all the book before you consider yourself competent. You may well find that some of the more advanced features have no relevance to your type of work, in which case, skip those sections and concentrate on those you need.

Chapters 2–8 cover the basics of word processing. However, some sophisticated features are tucked into Chapter 8, because they are formatting features.

Chapters 8–12 are what you could classify as intermediate features, and Chapters 13 and 14 are some of the more useful advanced features.

Chapter 15 has exercises for further practice of your newly acquired skills. We have deliberately not obscured the chapters instructing you how to use the word processing package with too much practice material, because we feel that you may wish to practise your skills on your own work.

Chapter 16 gives installation instructions for WordPerfect. A summary of the use of function keys and quick cursor movements, together with a glossary of computer terms, is given at the end of the book.

1.7 Installation information

If WordPerfect is not installed on your computer, you will need to consult chapter 16 of this book for detailed instructions on how to do this.

It is easier to work with WordPerfect installed within its own directory on a hard disk. Ensure that you are always in the WordPerfect directory before using the word processing package.

However, if you are using a computer with twin floppy disk drives, with no hard disk, you will have to remember to use drive A for the WordPerfect program and keep the program disk in it whilst you work. You will then use drive B for your work disks.

Do remember to take a backup copy of your program disks, in case of any future problems.

1.8 Work disks

Whether you have a twin floppy disk drive computer system or a computer with a hard disk installed, we suggest you store your work in files on a blank formatted disk. It is possible to store your work files on the hard disk, but it will probably be better if you save them on a floppy disk, so that you do not use valuable hard disk space for practice exercises. Keep the hard disk storage for computer work files you are going to want to use frequently, e.g. a standard letter which you will often want to use and just alter slightly.

1.9 Help facilities

WordPerfect is usually supplied with a template which you can attach to your keyboard. This explains the use of the function keys used alone or in conjunction with SHIFT, CTRL and ALT keys. This is most useful to have permanently adhered to your keyboard.

When you press F3, WordPerfect displays information about features of the package. You can either type a letter of the alphabet (A–Z) to see a list of all the features that begin with that letter or you can select a WordPerfect feature to see a screen of information about the feature. When you have obtained the information you require, you can press the SPACE BAR or ENTER to return to your document.

If you are using a twin floppy disk drive system, you may need to insert the WordPerfect 1 or WordPerfect 1/WordPerfect 2 disk (depending on whether you have 5.25″ or 3.5″ disks) into drive A and enter the drive letter.

After you have pressed the F3 function key to display Help, you can press it again to display a template of the keyboard, which summarises the use of the function keys. It will be similar, of course, to the template supplied with the package. So if you have lost the template, remember to press F3 twice to call up the keyboard template.

The template looks like screen dump 1.2.

A Quick Reference card is also supplied with WordPerfect which lists the features of the package and the keystrokes used to access those features. It does not supply detailed information but is useful as a memory jogger.

```
          WordPerfect 5.0 Template

          ┌──────────────────┬──────────────────┐
          │     Shell        │     Spell        │
    F1    │     SETUP        │   <-SEARCH       │ F2
          │   Thesaurus      │    Replace       │
          │    Cancel        │   Search->       │
          ├──────────────────┼──────────────────┤              Legend:
          │     Screen       │     Move         │
    F3    │     SWITCH       │  ->INDENT<-      │ F4
          │  Reveal Codes    │    Block         │    Ctrl + Function Key
          │     Help         │   ->Indent       │  SHIFT + FUNCTION KEY
          ├──────────────────┼──────────────────┤    Alt + Function Key
          │   Text In/Out    │   Tab Align      │    Function Key alone
    F5    │  DATE/OUTLINE    │    CENTRE        │ F6
          │   Mark Text      │  Flush Right     │
          │  List Files      │     Bold         │
          ├──────────────────┼──────────────────┤
          │    Footnote      │     Font         │
    F7    │     PRINT        │    FORMAT        │ F8
          │  Maths/Columns   │    Style         │
          │     Exit         │  Underline       │
          ├──────────────────┼──────────────────┤
          │   Merge/Sort     │  Macro Def.      │
    F9    │  MERGE CODES     │   RETRIEVE       │ F10
          │   Graphics       │    Macro         │
          │   Merge R        │    Save          │
          └──────────────────┴──────────────────┘
```

Screen Dump 1.2

1.10 Summary

In this chapter you have been introduced to the concepts of word processing and the use of WordPerfect. After working through this book, you should be a highly skilled user of WordPerfect and find it an enjoyable package to use on your computer.

Work through the book at your own pace, and refer back to earlier chapters where you need to refresh your memory of WordPerfect.

2 GETTING STARTED

In this section, you will learn how to start the WordPerfect program, create a new document, make insertions and deletions in your text and save the text on a disk.

2.1 Loading WordPerfect

Your brand new copy of WordPerfect will arrive in a pack containing probably eight floppy disks, a manual and a template. Before you switch on your computer, it would be simplest to ask your supplier how to install it and what the start-up routine is.

Basically, it will depend on whether your computer uses floppy or hard disk storage. If the former, a *copy* of the WordPerfect system disk will remain in the left-hand floppy disk drive (known as **drive A:**) during operation with your own work disk in the right hand floppy disk drive (known as **drive B:**). If your computer has a hard disk (known as **drive C:**) then there is usually only one floppy disk drive (drive A:) and a copy of the WordPerfect program is stored on the hard disk.

See chapter 16 for details on how to take a copy of the WordPerfect systems disks onto other floppy disks or onto the hard disk, as appropriate for your machine. (It is important that you never use the original floppy disks during operation as they may become irrecoverably damaged.) Because of the size of the program, which requires up to eight floppy disks for storage, copying the whole program onto a hard disk is obviously a simpler option. We would thus recommend you purchase a machine with its own hard disk to run a powerful program like WordPerfect.

The start-up procedure will also vary depending on whether you are using a floppy or hard disk machine.

Start by turning your computer on. You can now begin the start-up procedure.

Using twin floppy disk drives

In the case of a twin floppy disk drive, as you turn on the computer you will need to place a MSDOS disk in drive A:. When the contents of this disk are loaded an A:\> will appear on the lefthand side of the screen. You can then replace the MSDOS disk in the lefthand drive (A:) with the 5" WordPerfect system(s) disk. If your computer uses 3.5" disks you only need one system disk. If it uses 5.25" disks you have two system disks which you load one after the other. Place your formatted work disk in drive B:. When the A:\> prompt appears type 'B:' (without the inverted commas) and press ENTER. The B:\> prompt will appear. Type 'A:WP' and press ENTER. (Follow the screen prompts to replace the first system disk with the second if you are using 5.25" floppy disks.)

Using the hard disk

A machine with its own hard disk should start up when switched on without a floppy disk in the disk drive. The screen should display 'C:\>'. You will need to key in 'cd WP50' (if you are using version 5.0 of WordPerfect) and press ENTER. The prompt 'C:\WP50' will appear. If you are using version 5.1, key in 'cd WP51' and press ENTER and the prompt 'c:\WP51' will appear. If you have a hard disk system, make sure your screen prompt displays C:\WP50 or C:\WP51 before you go any further. Now you can type 'WP' and ENTER. The program will then be loaded.

Once loaded, your screen will look like sceen dump 2.1.

The 'blinking' line '_' (or a solid highlighted rectangle in version 5.1) is called the **cursor**, which indicates where you are currently working on the screen. This will move as you key in text or move around the screen with your **cursor keys**. These cursor keys are situated on the right hand side of the keyboard, and are marked with arrows pointing in the direction the cursor will move when these keys are pressed. You won't actually be able to move the cursor around the screen at this stage because you do not have any text displayed yet.

At the bottom right hand corner of the screen you will notice the **status line**. This displays (working from left to right) the document number, the page number, and the position on the page where you are currently working, which is defined by the row and column position

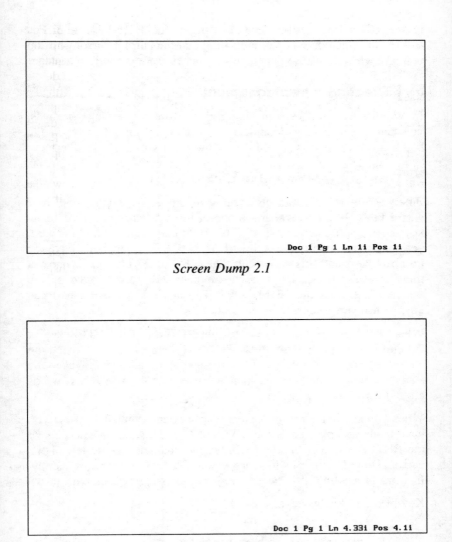

Doc 1 Pg 1 Ln 1i Pos 1i

Screen Dump 2.1

Doc 1 Pg 1 Ln 4.33i Pos 4.11

Screen Dump 2.1a

of the cursor in the selected unit of measurement, generally inches. In
other words, when the cursor is approximately half way down the page

13 ■

in the middle, the status line will display 'Doc 1 Pg 1 Ln 4.33i Pos 4.1i' as in screen dump 2.1a, indicating that the current cursor position is 4.33 inches down the page and 4.1 inches from the left-hand edge.

2.2 Creating a new document

In WordPerfect, unlike some other rival word processing packages, you can create a new document by keying in straightaway on the blank screen, which is presented to you when you load WordPerfect.

2.3 Cursor movement and wordwrap

Firstly, there is one note of warning at this stage when using your cursor keys. If your keyboard is one of those where the cursor arrow keys share the numeric keypad to the right hand side of the keyboard, you may inadvertently press the **NUM LOCK** key, situated above the up arrow key, and this will mean that every time you press what you think is a directional arrow key, a number will be displayed on the screen. Just press the NUM LOCK key again and the use of these keys will revert to cursor movement.

When word processing you do not need to press the ENTER key at the end of each line. Only press the ENTER key when you reach the end of the paragraph. As you type, the text automatically moves to the start of a new line. This is called **wordwrap** because the text wraps around from one line to the next.

When you key in the following text, if you notice immediately that you have made an error, press the BACKSPACE DEL key located above the ENTER key and this will remove the character to the left of the cursor. Do not worry about errors which you only notice subsequently. In word processing, it is quicker to leave your corrections until later.

Key in the following text:

```
Using a word processor saves the author time and trouble
and enables him or her to present work more
attractively than if a typewriter was used. The ease
with which corrections can be made encourages one to
be more creative since text can easily be altered.
```

As you type you will notice that the information given on the status line changes. The line and position measurements will change as the cursor moves on the screen.

You can now practise using the cursor keys, which are the four keys on the righthand side of the keyboard. If you move the key with the upward-pointing arrow, you will find that the cursor moves upwards in the text. Practise using all the cursor keys so that you get used to moving around in the text on your screen.

If you are using WordPerfect version 5.1 with a mouse, you can use the mouse to move the cursor around your work quickly. Roll the mouse across the surface of your desk until you have located the position you require with the pointer, then press the left button of the mouse to place the cursor.

Should you press the right mouse button when the pointer is on the screen, you will find that a menu bar will appear at the top of the screen. Pressing the right mouse button on any other words displayed in this menu bar will produce a drop down menu. We are not covering the use of these menus in this book, but when you have become competent with the package you will find them self-explanatory.

Spend some time at this before you move onto the next section.

2.4 Inserting and deleting characters _____

Word processing makes it very easy to insert and delete text either at the time of writing or at a later stage.

In WordPerfect to insert a character, word or sentence, position your cursor at the point where you wish the additional text to appear and type it in.

Using the exercise in section 2.3, position your cursor on the 't' of 'time' and type 'much' and press the spacebar. You will notice that the text automatically moves along to the right of the cursor to make room for the addition. Now position your cursor on the 't' of typewriter and type 'traditional'.

To delete characters using the BACKSPACE DEL key as mentioned in section 2.3, place your cursor on the character immediately after the text you wish to be deleted. The BACKSPACE DEL key will remove the character immediately to the left of the cursor.

Practise deleting characters now, by moving your cursor to the 'a' of 'attractively' , and press the BACKSPACE DEL key five times to remove the word and the space after it.

Practise inserting and deleting text now, by moving your cursor to the 't' of 'time' and press the backspace key until the words 'much', 'author' and 'the' disappear. Notice that the word 'time' has now moved up to follow 'saves'.

Now place your cursor on the 't' of 'time' and key in 'a writer' and press the spacebar.

The ability to insert and delete freely is one of the great advantages of word processing.

2.5 Saving text

If you need to save your text permanently for possible future use or modification, you will need to store it on a disk. Whenever you key in text and it appears on screen, it is temporarily stored in the computer's main memory. This text will be lost if you switch off or leave your word processing program.

Not all text will merit permanent storage, but it is useful to be able to retrieve work that you might want to edit and re-use later. Do not get into the habit of saving every little note, because computer storage, like any other, can become clogged with unnecessary filing.

It is a good working procedure to save text during a writing session, in case there is a power cut, or the machine is accidentally switched off, which would mean that you would lose all your text. In WordPerfect you have the choice of saving text before you leave the package or saving text and continuing to use the package.

To save the practice exercise from section 2.3, and at the same time clear your screen ready for keying-in the next task, press F7 and press 'y' to save.

You will be prompted by the computer to tell it where you want your work to be stored and what you want it to be called.

Filenames

Care must be taken with computer filenames. Each file must have a unique name because if you save a file using an existing file name of some old work, your latest file will write over the old file and the old file will be lost. Filenames should be a maximum of eight characters, with no spaces or punctuation in the title. They can be keyed in using either upper or lower case characters, but will always be converted to upper case by the package when displayed later on the screen.

If you are using a twin floppy disk drive, you will need to indicate the drive where your work disk is located, e.g. B:, followed by the filename you wish to use, e.g. your initials and the exercise number. Using this example, key in 'b:EX2A' and press the ENTER key. Key in 'N' to remain in WordPerfect when you are prompted by the computer.

If you have a hard disk, you have a choice of where to store your work. It can either be stored on the hard disk itself or on a floppy disk in the disk drive. The floppy disk drive will be given the letter 'A:' to identify it, and the hard disk will be 'C:'. The colon *always* has to be keyed in after the drive letter and before the filename is typed. Therefore to save on a hard disk you will need to key in 'C:EX2A'. To use the single floppy disk drive of a hard disk system, key in 'A:EX2A'.

Using the F10 function key is another very useful way to save your text as you go along and avoid accidentally losing it. This facility allows you to save the work you have done so far but leaves your current task loaded ready to be continued.

You merely press F10 and if it is the first time you are saving the document, key in 'B:EX2A' or whichever drive letter is the most appropriate to you. If you have already saved it, then the filename you used will appear on screen. You can press the ENTER key, and say 'Y' to replace the previous version. In other words, the most recent work replaces the previously stored version.

Do make sure you save your work as you go, in case of power failure. It is infuriating to lose everything you have done if the machine is accidentally switched off.

2.6 Practice

You will now have a blank screen after completing the instructions given before, so you can practise some of the features you have learned.

Key in the following text. Press the ENTER key twice to create a new paragraph. This leaves a space between paragraphs.

```
Filing with a computer is similar to placing papers in
a filing cabinet. In other words, you need to be able
to find things quickly and easily. To facilitate this,
get in the habit of using filenames which will organise
your work in a way which is meaningful and helpful to
you. Do not be tempted to use filenames which do not
relate to the work being stored.

A common fault of beginners is to use a filename which
is either too long, is broken-up with spaces and
punctuation, or is frivolous. To be acceptable to the
computer a filename must not be longer than eight
characters and must only contain letters or numbers,
e.g. cttee1 (which could be the minutes of the first
committee meeting held).

The computer needs to know which disk to store the file
on. You will need to specify the drive name by keying
in the appropriate identifying letter, followed by a
colon, followed by the filename, i.e. A:cttee1.
```

Check your document through for any errors, and correct them using the BACKSPACE DEL key or by inserting any omissions.

Save it under the filename 'Ex2B' using the appropriate drive letter (e.g. A:EX2B).

Then make the following changes to the text:

1 Delete the word 'things' in the first paragraph and replace it with the word 'documents'.

2 Delete the word 'organise' in the first paragraph and replace it with the word 'arrange'.

3 At the end of the first paragraph insert ', or are frivolous'.

4 In the second paragraph delete ', or is frivolous'.

5 In the third paragraph after 'appropriate identifying letter,' insert 'which is likely to be A, B, or C,'.

Your document should now look like this.

```
Filing with a computer is similar to placing papers in
a filing cabinet. In other words, you need to be able
to find documents quickly and easily. To facilitate
this, get in the habit of using filenames which will
arrange your work in a way which is meaningful and
helpful to you. Do not be tempted to use filenames
which do not relate the the work being stored, or are
frivolous.

A common fault of beginners is to use a filename which
is either too long, is broken-up with spaces and
punctuation. To be acceptable to the computer a
filename must not be longer than eight characters and
must only contain letters or numbers, e.g. cttee1
(which could be the minutes of the first committee
meeting held).

The computer needs to know which disk to store the file
on. You will need to specify the drive name by keying
in the appropriate identifying letter, this is likely
to be A, B or C, followed by a colon, followed by the
filename, i.e. A:cttee1.
```

2.7 Quitting WordPerfect

To leave WordPerfect, press F7, answer 'Y' to save this document, type your filename e.g. 'A:EX2C' and press the ENTER key. Type 'Y' to exit the package.

Be sure to take out any floppy disks before you switch off your machine. If you do not do this, you may risk damaging your disks.

2.8 Cancel key

A very useful key to mention at this stage is the **Cancel** key. You will notice that at bottom right hand side of the screen, after you have saved a document and when you are prompted about leaving WordPerfect or not, you are also offered the opportunity to cancel and return to the document just saved. F1 is the key used to cancel a command you have just given. This is one occasion when it is used but you will find there are many other times when it will prove a very useful facility.

2.9 Retrieving saved text

To retrieve saved text, you first of all load the package WordPerfect as described in section 2.1. To find your list of files, press F5 and the ENTER key. A list of files is displayed. There will also be a menu at the bottom of the screen offering various options. This is shown in the screen dump below.

```
12/10/90  08:06              Directory A:\*.*
Document size:      721   Free:  1411584   Used:      40612        Files:  24

. <CURRENT>    <DIR>              .. <PARENT>    <DIR>
EX10A   .       7134  05/10/90 09:20    EX12A   .       1520  07/10/90 07:46
EX12B   .       1557  07/10/90 07:47    EX12C   .       2390  07/10/90 07:49
EX12D   .       1664  07/10/90 07:51    EX12E   .       2927  07/10/90 07:54
EX13A   .       3370  07/10/90 08:00    EX2A    .        877  05/10/90 08:19
EX2B    .       1522  05/10/90 08:24    EX2C    .       2150  05/10/90 08:29
EX3A    .       1041  05/10/90 08:35    EX5A    .       1123  05/10/90 08:38
EX5B    .        875  05/10/90 08:39    EX5C    .       1020  05/10/90 08:42
EX6A    .       1332  05/10/90 08:46    EX6C    .       1147  05/10/90 08:49
EX7A    .       1170  05/10/90 08:56    EX7B    .       1082  05/10/90 08:59
EX7C    .       1253  05/10/90 09:03    EX7D    .        860  05/10/90 09:05
EX8A    .        943  05/10/90 09:08    EX9A    .        996  05/10/90 09:11
EX9B    .       1816  07/10/90 07:56    EX9C    .        843  05/10/90 09:14




1 Retrieve; 2 Delete; 3 Move/Rename; 4 Print; 5 Text In;
6 Look; 7 Other Directory; 8 Copy; 9 Word Search; N Name Search: 6
```

Screen Dump 2.2

Move the cursor to highlight the filename you wish to retrieve, which in this case will be EX2C, and press either 'R' or '1'. You will notice that WordPerfect gives you the option to retrieve files either by using the first letter of the menu choice (i.e. R for Retrieve) or by pressing a number (i.e. 1).

This will display the previously stored document on screen ready for editing.

Your status line which we mentioned in section 2.1 will now display the drive, directory and filename you are using at the bottom left-hand corner of the screen.

```
Filing with a computer is similar to placing papers in a
filing cabinet. In other words, you need to be able to find
documents quickly and easily. To facilitate this, get in the
habit of using filenames which will arrange your work in a way
which is meaningful and helpful to you. Do not be tempted to
use filenames which do not relate to the work being stored or
are frivolous.

A common fault of beginners is to use a filename which is
either too long, is broken-up with spaces and punctuation. To
be acceptable to the computer a filename must not be longer
than 8 characters and must only contain letters or numbers, eg
cttee1 (which could be the minutes of the first committee
meeting held).

The computer needs to know which disk to store the file on.
You will need to specify the drive name by keying in the
appropriate identifying letter, this is likely to be A, B, or
C, followed by a colon, followed by the filename, ie A:cttee1.



A:\EX2C                                    Doc 1 Pg 1 Ln 1i Pos 1i
```

Screen Dump 2.3

2.10 Retrieving text from floppy disk _____

In section 2.5, you learned how to save your text both on the hard disk or on a floppy disk. Floppy disks can be a useful storage medium, even if your computer is provided with a hard disk. You can take disks elsewhere to print or in order to work on other machines. You can make backup copies of important or confidential work. You can lock up a floppy disk, without having to resort to passwords on the hard disk, which might cause you problems if you forget the password.

However, working and filing is considerably faster on hard disk. In most cases documents are saved on the hard disk with backup (duplicate) copies on floppy disks.

To retrieve any stored work, you first of all press F5. The screen prompt which appears will depend on which drives your computer uses and how WordPerfect has been installed. If you are using hard disk storage the words 'C:\WP*.*' will appear, However, if WordPerfect has been instructed at installation to use floppy disk storage then 'A:*.*' will be appear as a screen prompt. On the other hand, if you are using twin floppy disk drives for your storage, 'B:*.*' will appear on the screen. Then you have a choice of either accepting the default drive (the drive WordPerfect is automatically instructed to select), or overwriting the default drive if your work is stored elsewhere.

If you wish to select the displayed default drive, press ENTER. However, should you wish to select a drive other than the default displayed at the screen prompt, you just type in the drive you require followed by a colon and press ENTER , e.g. 'B:' and then ENTER. Alternatively, you may wish to alter the default drive for your current session, which is done by pressing '=' and entering 'B:' then ENTER. This will remain in force until you switch your machine off.

Having chosen your drive, you will see on screen a directory (which means a list) of your files. Move the cursor until the file you wish to work on is highlighted, (for version 5.1 you can take your mouse pointer to the required file and select it by pressing the left mouse button) and press '1' to retrieve the file onto the screen. It is now ready for you to work on.

A quick and easy way of retrieving your work if you know the file-name, is to press SHIFT and F10, and you will be prompted 'Document to be retrieved:' in the bottom left corner. Key in the name and press ENTER and the document will appear on screen. If it is in a different disk drive, from the one you are working in, you will need to specify that too, e.g. 'B:EX2C'.

2.11 Clearing the screen ──────────────

You will often find that you do not need to keep minor notes and personal letters which you have keyed in and printed. Once you are sure you have a satisfactory final copy, you may merely wish to clear your screen ready for writing something else.

To clear your screen, without saving your document, press F7 to exit and type 'N' to show that you do not want to save the personal note, and then 'N' not to come out of WordPerfect.

Practise loading in the exercises you completed earlier using the file-names EX2A, EX2B, EX2C and clear your screen between each operation as described above.

2.12 Looking at file contents ──────────────

When you have your directory of files on screen, you can quickly see what is in the file by pressing ENTER. This will show you the text but will *not* retrieve it for you to work on. When you have finished looking at the contents, press the exit key, F7, to return to the directory of files.

If it is the file you want, you must remember to press '1' to retrieve it when the directory of files is displayed on screen. It can be an easy mistake to keep pressing ENTER each time you highlight a filename and then wondering why you cannot work on it. On the other hand, this can avoid loading the wrong file and having to clear your screen.

You can practise this facility using your three practice exercises which you filed under the names EX2A, EX2B, EX2C. As you do this you will find you can read the text but not edit it in any way.

2.13 Further practice ──────────────

If you feel you need to practise the features of WordPerfect described in this chapter before moving on, the following exercise is provided. Key in this passage from George Bernard Shaw.

```
If you are learning English because you intend to
travel in England and wish to be understood there, do
not try to speak English perfectly, because, if you do,
```

no one will understand you.

No foreigner can ever stress the syllables and make the
voice rise and fall in question and answer, assertion
and denial, refusal and consent, exactly as a native
does.

Therefore the first thing you have to do is to speak
with a strong foreign accent, and speak broken English:
that is, English without grammar. Then every English
person to whom you speak will at once know that you are
a foreigner, and try to understand you and be ready to
help you. He will not expect you to be polite and to
use elaborate grammatical phrases. He will be
interested in you because you are a stranger, and
pleased by his own cleverness in making out your
meaning and being able to tell you what you want to
know.

1. Save it as EX2D in the way described in 2.5 above and quit Word-
Perfect.

2. Re-load WordPerfect and examine the contents of file EX2D, without actually retrieving it (see 2.12). Having reassured yourself that this
is the file that requires editing, retrieve it, following the instructions
given in 2.9 and 2.10.

3. Now you are ready to edit the text. Delete the word 'England' in
the first paragraph and replace it with 'English-speaking world'.

4. Delete the word 'foreigner' in the second paragraph and replace it
with 'one from overseas'.

5. In the third paragraph delete the words 'he' and 'his' and replace
them with 'she' and 'hers'.

6. Quit WordPerfect when you have made these changes but do not
save this edited version unless you really want it. It's probably not an
improvement on the original!

2.14 Summary ——————————————————————————

In this chapter you have learned how to

- load WordPerfect
- create a new document
- insert and delete text
- save your work
- quit WordPerfect
- retrieve saved work
- clear your screen

3 PRINTING AND EDITING DOCUMENTS

In this chapter you will learn how to produce printed copies of documents, whether you have saved them or not, and also how to delete text and make changes in the paragraphing.

If you have turned off the computer since using Chapter 2, you will need to re-load WordPerfect (see section 2.1 on how to load the word processing package) and retrieve text, which is covered in section 2.8.

Sections 3.2 (Printing a page) and 3.3 (Printing from a file) will be more useful to you when you are working on chapter 10, Long Documents, but for ease of reference all the printing facilities are grouped together.

3.1 Printing a current document

You can print a document which is displayed on the screen, or one which is saved on a disk. You can also print a document which has already been saved on disk, whilst you are editing another document, in section 3.3 (although you are unlikely to use this facility until you are more familar with WordPerfect). This means that you can be working on a document whilst another one is being printed. This is called background printing and it enables full use to be made of both the printer and the computer terminal.

Before printing, check that your printer is switched on and if it has a light panel, labelled **on-line**, check it is illuminated (which means the printer is connected to the computer), and that paper is ready for use, either inserted between the rollers or in the paper tray. Paper should only be handled in the printer when it is **off-line**, which means that it is in local mode and can be adjusted like a typewriter, rather than under the control of the computer. Continuous stationery, in particular, needs to be carefully loaded and the **line-feed** (moving the paper up one line at a time) and **form-feed** (moving the paper up one page at a time) operations should be tested before putting the printer on-line.

To print a document which is displayed on the screen, first of all retrieve the work you did in chapter 2. To retrieve text, press the F5 key (List Files) and press the ENTER key. A list of files/documents is displayed. Move the cursor to highlight the filename, (e.g. EX2C) and press either 'R' for Retrieve or '1' from the menu at the bottom of the list.

Once the text is displayed on the screen, hold the SHIFT key down and press F7. This will display the print menu (as shown in the screen dump below). Select '1' (Full Document) so that the whole document will be sent to the printer.

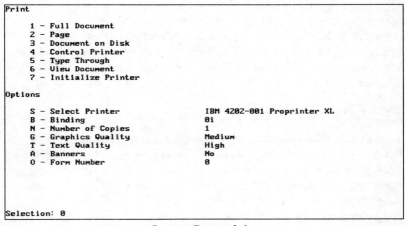

```
Print

    1 - Full Document
    2 - Page
    3 - Document on Disk
    4 - Control Printer
    5 - Type Through
    6 - View Document
    7 - Initialize Printer

Options

    S - Select Printer              IBM 4202-001 Proprinter XL
    B - Binding                     0i
    N - Number of Copies            1
    G - Graphics Quality            Medium
    T - Text Quality                High
    A - Banners                     No
    O - Form Number                 0




Selection: 0
```

Screen Dump 3.1

You can follow the above procedure to print text displayed on your computer screen, whether you have saved it or not. This is useful for printing out letters or notes which you do not need to save.

You now need to press the function key marked F7 to clear your screen, answer 'N' to the question 'Save document? (Y/N)', since it is already saved, and 'N' to the question 'Exit WP? (Y/N)', so that you are presented with a blank screen ready for keying in some fresh text to practise insertions and deletions.

3.2 Printing a page

It can be useful to print just one page from a document, particularly when you are typing long documents. To do this, move the cursor to the page that you want printed, press SHIFT and F7 (the Print option), and type '2' (the Page option). The page will then be printed.

3.3 Printing from a file

You may be working on one document and decide you would like to have a printed copy of another document to refer to. You can print this without having to load the file concerned.

Press SHIFT and F7 (the Print option), and type '3' (the Document on Disk option). Key in the name of the file you want to print, if necessary specifying the drive where it is stored, e.g. 'C:\WP\filename', and press ENTER. You will be prompted 'Page(s)(All)' which gives the opportunity to specify the pages you want printed. Press ENTER to select the whole document or key in the page numbers you require, e.g. 1,3 (for pages 1 and 3) or if it is a range of pages, type '2.5'.

3.4 Deleting characters at the cursor

Key in the following text so that you have a passage on which to practise editing, and save it as EX3A. You may wish to use the **CAPS LOCK** facility to key in the word VDU in the passage. When you press the key marked CAPS LOCK all the text will be in capitals. After keying in the word 'VDU', press CAPS LOCK again and any following text will revert to lower case letters. This is called a **toggle** key. This means that you press it once to activate the function, and press it again to switch it off.

```
A computer system consists of hardware and
software. The term hardware means all physical,
electronic and mechanical elements forming part of
the computer system, and software is another word
for the instructions or programs which the hardware
needs to function.

Hardware usually comprises the following:-
```

Keyboard

Visual Display Unit (VDU)

Monitor or screen

Disk Drive

Printer

Mouse (possibly)

Central Processing Unit

You learned how to use the BACKSPACE DELETE key in Chapter 2. This key deletes the character immediately to the left of the cursor.

An alternative way of deleting is to use the key marked **DEL**. This will delete the character immediately at (i.e. above) the cursor position. Move your cursor to the start of the word 'monitor'. Press the DEL Key repeatedly and the word will disappear character by character into the computer's temporary memory.

You will notice that the text automatically closes up as you delete a character, unlike typing.

3.5 Deleting words and lines _____

The above method is fine for a single character, but more likely you will want to delete whole words or even lines. Move your cursor to the start of the word 'screen' and hold down the CTRL key and press BACKSPACE. Notice the whole word disappears. If you have placed your cursor on a space, then the word to the left of the cursor will have disappeared.

Place your cursor at the start of the line 'Visual Display Unit'and press CTRL and END together. Notice that the whole line is erased. If you want the text to close up, so that a blank line is not left, you will need to press the BACKSPACE DEL key to erase the line return that had been inserted when the text was keyed in.

3.6 Deleting to end of page

You may, at times, need to delete text from a specific point to the end of the page. To practise this, move your cursor to the word 'Hardware' and press CTRL and PGDN. The message 'Delete Remainder of Page? (Y/N) No' will now appear on screen. (This is again an example of the safe default mentioned in section 1.1, whereby the user could not delete anything in error by thoughtlessly pressing ENTER.) Type 'Y' to delete the text.

3.7 Correcting unwanted deletions

If, using the above methods, you immediately change your mind after you have deleted some text, just press F1 to bring up a small **Undelete** menu, and then press 1 (Restore) and the text is restored.

However, with WordPerfect you have the facility to bring back the *last* three deletions you have made. These deletions are stored in what is known as a buffer, which is like a temporary, small memory reserved for this purpose.

To use this facility, first press F1, which is the cancel key, and then press '2' (Previous Deletion) up to three times to show the three stored deletions. When the stored deletion required is shown, press '1' (Restore) to restore it. Now practise this function and restore the last two deletions you have made.

3.8 Paragraph break

When editing text, one often wants to break text into more manageable chunks for reading. This is very simple with all word processing packages. Move your cursor to the first character of the sentence you wish to start your new paragraph, and press the ENTER key twice. It is customary to leave one blank line between paragraphs to make for easier reading and better layout.

Now try it by moving your cursor to the start of the sentence beginning 'The term' and press the ENTER key twice. You will see that in

WordPerfect the text automatically moves down to make room for these returns.

3.9 Paragraph combine and codes

Alternatively, you may wish to combine paragraphs, which you had previously divided. Here, WordPerfect helps you with codes, which are normally hidden. If you press the key marked ALT and the F3 key (ALT-F3) or F11 alternatively, these codes will be revealed by means of a split screen, showing text as it normally appears in the top half and the same text in the bottom half of the screen with reveal codes shown. They are not printed out, but are there to help you with editing.

When you press ALT-F3, your screen will look like screen dump 3.2. The facility which you have just used is known as **Reveal Codes**.

```
Filing with a computer is similar to placing papers in a
filing cabinet. In other words, you need to be able to find
documents quickly and easily. To facilitate this, get in the
habit of using filenames which will arrange your work in a way
which is meaningful and helpful to you. Do not be tempted to
use filenames which do not relate to the work being stored or
are frivolous.

A common fault of beginners is to use a filename which is
either too long, is broken-up with spaces and punctuation. To
be acceptable to the computer a filename must not be longer
A:\EX2C                                    Doc 1 Pg 1 Ln 2.33i Pos 1i
(                                                                    )
are frivolous.[HRt]
[HRt]
A common fault of beginners is to use a filename which is[SRt]
either too long, is broken[-]up with spaces and punctuation. To[SRt]
be acceptable to the computer a filename must not be longer[SRt]
than 8 characters and must only contain letters or numbers, eg[SRt]
cttee1 (which could be the minutes of the first committee[SRt]
meeting held).[HRt]
[HRt]
The computer needs to know which disk to store the file on.[SRt]

Press Reveal Codes to restore screen
```

Screen Dump 3.2

You can now see very clearly where you pressed the ENTER key to end a paragraph as it is coded '[HRt]'. This will prove most useful if you decide you want to combine paragraphs.

'HRt' is the WordPerfect code for a **hard return** which is when the keyboard operator decides the line should end rather than leaving it up to the Wordwrap facility of the package. Incidentally, the line ending dictated by the wordwrap facility is known as a **soft return** and this will show up on screen as the code '[SRt]'.

Move your cursor so that it is over the '[HRt]' code after the full stop at the end of the paragraph finishing with the word 'function' and press the DEL key twice. You will see that the two paragraphs have now become one with the removal of the two '[HRt]' codes.

Press ALT-F3 to turn off the split screen facility and return your screen to its normal appearance.

3.10 Revision

Save your text now by pressing F10 to save this document. Type EX3A (preceded by either 'A:' or 'B:' if you are using a floppy disk for storage) and press ENTER. Type 'N' to remain in WordPerfect.

Now print out your work by pressing Shift-F7, choose 1 (Full Document) from the print menu, and then press F7 to exit this sub-menu.

To exit the WordPerfect package, press F7, type 'N' when you have the 'Save' message displayed because you have just saved the document, and type 'Y' to exit WordPerfect.

3.11 Practice

Should you need to practise the facilities described in this chapter again, key in the following passage and save it as EX3B.

```
We are all aware of the increase during this
century of cardio-vascular disease - bitter fruit
of anxiety, stress and excessive speed. We are
perhaps less aware that a company located in
Neuchatel, Switzerland shares, with its American
parent, a dominant position in the manufacturing of
cardiac pacemakers and accessories necessary for
their functioning.

After centuries of mastering rhythm in connection
with time, Neuchatel's watch and clock makers today
```

```
have also applied their expertise to the adjustment
of man's failing biological rhythm. Future
developments at this Swiss plant also include
research into replacement of defective human organs.
```

1. Make a paragraph break beginning 'We are perhaps less', but combine the paragraph beginning 'After centuries'with the previous one. (See 3.8 and 3.9.)

2. Delete the word 'American' in the second paragraph using the DEL key and also delete the entire last sentence of the passage (see 3.6).

3. However, on reflection, you should restore the word 'American' (see 3.7).

4. Save your text again and clear the screen.

5. Now print this file (EX3B) without reloading it (see 3.3).

3.12 Summary

You should now be able to carry out a whole range of editing functions, including different ways of deleting text, breaking and combining paragraphs, printing out copies, and saving and retrieving text. If you are unsure of these functions, practise them on text of your own before you continue.

4 FILE OPERATIONS

4.1 Changing disk drive

In Chapter 2, you were shown how to retrieve saved work from disk. It may be that you usually save your work on a floppy disk, but wish to get at some work on the hard disk. You therefore need to change disk drive.

To do this, press F5 to retrieve your work. Then press '=' (equals sign) and then 'C:' for the hard disk drive, or 'B:' if you are using twin floppy drives. Alternatively, you can just key in the required drive name 'B:' or 'C:', and press ENTER twice to get a directory (list) of your files.

There is another way of changing your disk drive. If, after you have pressed F5 and got a list of files on one drive, you find that the file you are seeking is not there, you can choose 7 from the Status Line menu, and overtype the letter of the drive, followed by a colon, and press ENTER twice.

4.2 Copying files and making backups

For backup purposes, it can be useful to have a duplicate copy of your file. All important files should have a duplicate copy, in case the disk storing them becomes damaged accidentally. Also, if you wish to work in another location, it can be useful to have a duplicate copy to work on. *Remember even hard disks can fail and you could lose important work if you have not made a backup copy.*

To make a copy of a file, press F5 which will display on screen the current directory of files. It could be 'A':, 'B:' or 'C:', depending which files you wish to copy. If you need to change drives, see section 4.1.

Move the cursor to the filename(s) you wish to copy. If you want to copy more than one at a time mark each file with an asterisk. Press

'8' to enable you to choose 'copy' from the Status Line menu.

You will then be prompted 'Copy marked files? (Y/N) N'. Type 'Y' for yes and then the screen will display the message 'Copy all marked files to:'; enter the drive you want to copy these files onto (A, B, or C, don't forget the colon) and finally press ENTER to carry out this copying function.

Incidentally, if you want to unmark a file on a list, just move your cursor to the filename and press the asterisk key again. The star symbol disappears.

4.3 Deleting files

Filing is never a very exciting occupation and computer filing is no exception. Many word processor users get into a terrible muddle with this and have dreadful problems trying to retrieve a particular document. One of the major causes for this can be that the filing system is clogged up with old files that no one will ever want to look at again. Don't be afraid to throw out old files by deleting them.

Follow the above procedure to access a list of files for the appropriate drive, mark all the files you wish to remove in the same way, then press '2' (Delete) at the Status Line menu. A screen message will appear 'Delete marked files? (Y/N) No', type Y and a helpful message will appear to prevent you from making a terrible mistake, 'Marked files will be deleted. Continue? (Y/N) No'. Again the default is presented in such a way that files will not be accidentally deleted by carelessly pressing the ENTER key. When you have finished tidying up your files (called **housekeeping**), press F7 to exit.

4.4 Changing and moving filenames

It can be useful to rename files to make them more meaningful or to categorise them more appropriately. Yet again the same procedure is followed to access the list of files, but this time press '3' (Move/Rename) at the Status Line menu. With version 5.1, you will be presented with the screen message 'Move marked files? No (Yes)'. Answer 'N', and then follow the instructions below for changing the name. For version 5.0, this question will not be asked.

You will be presented with something like the following: 'New name: C:\wp\filename'. Move your cursor to the first character beyond the filename and delete all the characters back to the '\'. Now key in the new filename. It is also possible to move it to another disk drive by keying in the appropriate drive (i.e. B:).

Practise this by altering the existing file EX2C, to make it 'LESSON2'. When you have altered this, look at your file directory to view this changed filename, then change it back to its old filename of EX2C.

4.5 Creating directories for your files _____

To avoid the necessity for some of the laborious housekeeping tasks described above, it would be a better idea to do a bit of planning in advance. Decide on the general topics you will want to file your work under and set up directories on your storage disks in advance.

A directory in computing terms is a way of keeping categories of files tidily together. It is the equivalent of grouping files in a separate drawer in a filing cabinet. It is customary to group together files covering a specific area/topic. An example of this would be to have one directory to cover all personal letters, another directory for business letters, and a third for minutes of meetings.

To do this press F5 at the blank screen, type '=', then enter the name of the new directory, not forgetting the drive it has been created on, for example, 'A:Plan'. This would be suitable to store all work connected with a planning committee. You will be prompted with a message 'Create Plan? (Y/N) No'. Type 'Y' and the directory will be created. Your screen will look like screen dump 4.1.

To use this directory on subsequent occasions follow a similar procedure as for section 4.1. Press F5, type '=' and key in the pathname (e.g. 'A:\Plan'). By typing this, you are telling the computer where to look for your file by specifying the drive name followed by the directory name, separating the path signposts by a backslash (\).

Study screen dump 4.2.

Notice at the top, the directory name is given: 'Directory A:\PLAN*.*'. This means that the disk currently being used for storage is in the A

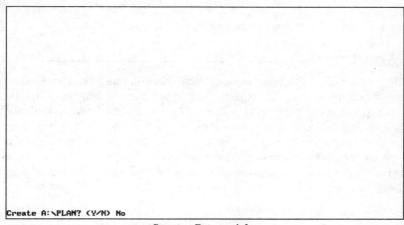

Create A:\PLAN? (Y/N) No

Screen Dump 4.1

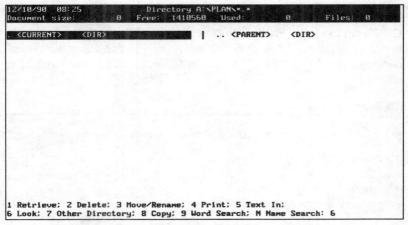

```
12/10/90  08:25              Directory A:\PLAN\*.*
Document size:       0   Free:  1410560   Used:        0        Files:  0
. <CURRENT>    <DIR>                    |   .. <PARENT>    <DIR>
```

```
1 Retrieve; 2 Delete; 3 Move/Rename; 4 Print; 5 Text In;
6 Look; 7 Other Directory; 8 Copy; 9 Word Search; N Name Search: 6
```

Screen Dump 4.2

drive, the directory (or storage area) is PLAN, and the *.* indicates
that the entire contents of this directory are being displayed on the

screen below.

Directory names are always converted into upper case by WordPerfect, even if keyed in in lower case, as you will have noticed.

4.6 Using DOS

DOS stands for **disk operating system**. No computer can run without an operating system. It is a computer program which links up the software (e.g. WordPerfect) with hardware, such as the keyboard, the screen and the printer. If your computer has a hard disk, the operating system is already installed on it and is activated automatically when you switch on the computer. However, if you have a twin floppy disk drive computer, you will know by now that you have to insert your DOS disk into the A: drive as you turn on.

DOS is used by experienced computer users to carry out such functions as copying and deleting files, instead of the way just described. Sometimes it is quicker to use DOS commands for your housekeeping etc., if you know them. DOS commands are not covered in this book, because they are adequately covered in numerous computer books.

However, WordPerfect offers you the facility to drop through to the DOS level to enter a DOS command. Press CTRL and F1 and you will find yourself at the DOS level. At this point you can enter appropriate commands and type 'EXIT' to return to WordPerfect when you have finished.

4.7 Summary

In this chapter you have learned about filing including

- copying files
- deleting files
- renaming files
- creating directories

The importance of good computer housekeeping has been stressed. If you follow the recommendations of this chapter, you should find the task of retrieving files simple, which is, after all, the proof that the filing system is working.

5 ALTERING THE APPEARANCE OF A DOCUMENT

You have already learned how to edit text by inserting and deleting, and now you will learn another basic way of editing text. This is by overtyping, and altering the overall appearance of your text using the centring, justification, alter margins and line-spacing facilities.

5.1 Use of overtype

Overtyping has a very limited use but, nevertheless, can be a useful facility for changing text of equal length, and particularly in altering columns of figures. Normally a word processing package is in insert mode all the time and as you key in, the cursor automatically moves along to make room for the text.

Key in the following passage of text, saving it as EX5A – if you make a mistake, you can practise your editing techniques learned in the last chapter.

```
Many people in business no longer communicate by
telephone or by posting a letter, but use fax machines.
The fax machine takes a document at one end of a
telephone line, and reproduces it at the receiver's end.
Fax can even be used for legal documents, drawings,
sketches of fashion designs, as well as for ordinary
business correspondence.

Using fax, the sender keeps a copy on paper of what has
been sent, and the receiver has the duplicate version to
look at or read, within seconds of it being sent.
```

Now you can practise the **overtype** facility. Take your cursor to 'Many' in the first paragraph, and press the INS key. You are now in **Typeover** mode, which is the term WordPerfect uses instead of overtype. The word **'Typeover'** is displayed on the left of the Status Line.

Type the word 'Lots' and press the INS key again. This action turns off the Typeover mode and returns you to the normal Insert mode. Now press the spacebar and type the word 'of' to come after the word 'lots'. This will show you two methods of editing, overtype and insert.

Now take your cursor to the word 'posting' and using the typeover facility, replace it with 'sending'. Continue to practise this by making the following replacements:

'reproduces' with 'duplicates'; 'even' with 'also'; 'ordinary' with 'standard'; 'keeps' with 'holds'; 'duplicate' with 'identical'; and 'look at' with 'examine'.

Practise deletion, by deleting 'or read'. You can either do this using BACKSPACE DEL (section 3.2) or word deletion (section 3.3).

5.2 Centring text

Some text looks much more attractive if you centre it. This centring facility is most frequently used for the main heading of a document, for items like menus and invitations where display is of paramount importance.

Save the text above as EX5A, clear your screen (section 2.9), and key in the following menu, pressing SHIFT and F6 at the start of each line. This command centres the text. When you press ENTER at the end of the line, this removes the centring instruction, which is why you *must* press SHIFT and F6 at the start of *each* line.

```
                    TODAY'S MENU


                  Soup of the Day
                  Prawn Cocktail
               Avocado Vinaigrette


                   Coq au Vin
                  Steak Tartare
                  Dover Sole
```

```
                    Sweets from the Trolley
                    Cheese Board

                    Coffee and Mints
```

Save the menu under the filename EX5B.

You may decide you do not want the menu centred after you have seen it. To remove the centring instructions, place the cursor on the first character at the start of the line to be uncentred, and press the BACKSPACE. Repeat this for each line, until the whole menu is aligned at the left margin.

Alternatively, you can centre a left-aligned section of text subsequently by pressing SHIFT and F6 at the start of the line or heading you wish to be centred.

Practise moving your menu from centred to left-aligned text, until you feel happy about using this display facility.

5.3 Line spacing

There is often a need to display text in such a way as to make it very easy to read. Examples of this are literary work, such as authors' manuscripts, theses, draft work, and press releases. When producing this type of work, double line spacing is almost invariably used.

Before you key in the text below, clear your screen and make sure your cursor is at the start of the new file. While holding SHIFT press F8, and the **Format** Menu appears — as shown in screen dump 5.1.

Press '1' to access Line Menu and then select '6' for Line Spacing. The cursor is at the point of entry for the spacing required, so type '2' and ENTER. Your screen should match screen dump 5.2.

Press F7 to get back to your document.

From now on your text will be in double line spacing, until you repeat the procedure above, to return it to single line spacing, by typing '1'.

Should you wish to use 1.5 line spacing, key in '1.5', or triple line spacing, key in '3' against '6 - Line spacing'.

```
Format
      1 - Line
                 Hyphenation                      Line Spacing
                 Justification                    Margins Left/Right
                 Line Height                      Tab Set
                 Line Numbering                   Widow/Orphan Protection

      2 - Page
                 Centre Page (top to bottom)      New Page Number
                 Force Odd/Even Page              Page Number Position
                 Headers and Footers              Paper Size/Type
                 Margins Top/Bottom               Suppress

      3 - Document
                 Display Pitch                    Redline Method
                 Initial Settings                 Summary

      4 - Other
                 Advance                          Overstrike
                 Conditional End of Page          Printer Functions
                 Decimal Characters               Underline Spaces/Tabs
                 Language

Selection: 0
```

Screen Dump 5.1

```
Format: Line
      1 - Hyphenation                          Off

      2 - Hyphenation Zone - Left              10%
                            Right              4%

      3 - Justification                        Yes

      4 - Line Height                          Auto

      5 - Line Numbering                       No

      6 - Line Spacing                         2

      7 - Margins - Left                       1i
                    Right                      1i

      8 - Tab Set                              0i, every 0.5i

      9 - Widow/Orphan Protection              No


Selection: 0
```

Screen Dump 5.2

Key in the text below and save it as EX5C.

```
OPENING OF NEW HOSPITAL WING

The Mayor, Councillor Mrs Wilson, opened the long-
awaited Neo-Natal Intensive Care Unit at the Royal
County Hospital on Saturday, 28 May. In her speech, the
Mayor highlighted the life-saving aspect of this new
unit, as newborn babies and their mothers would no
longer have to travel 20 miles to avail themselves of
these specialist care facilities in future.
```

Now centre the heading to this article in order to practise your centring (section 5.2).

5.4 Justifying text

A further embellishment to text layout often used in press releases, is to justify text, which means that the passage concerned has even left and right margins, instead of having an uneven right margin.

Take your cursor to the beginning of the passage you keyed in under section 5.3 (EX5C), and press SHIFT and F8. As in section 5.3, you will be presented with the Format Menu. Again, choose the Line Menu by pressing '1'. This time, choose option '3', and ensure 'Yes' is displayed alongside 'Justification'. Press F7 twice to return you to your document.

In version 5.1 of WordPerfect there is one extra step in the procedure described above. At the Format: Line menu check that at option 3 'Justification Full' is displayed. If not select '3' and a sub-menu will appear at the bottom of the screen: 'Justification: 1 Left; 2 Centre; 3 Right; 4 Full: 0'. Select '4' (Full) if you wish both your right and left margins to be justified.

You will find that your document remains unchanged on screen. However, it will be justified when you print it.

It is possible to view it, however, by choosing the View Document facility, which is described in the next section.

Your printed document will look like this.

OPENING OF NEW HOSPITAL WING

The Mayor, Councillor Mrs Wilson, opened the
long-awaited Neo-Natal Intensive Care Unit at the
Royal County Hospital on Saturday, 28 May. In her
speech, the Mayor highlighted the life-saving
aspect of this new unit, as newborn babies and
their mothers would no longer have to travel 20
miles to avail themselves of these specialist
care facilities in future.

It may be that the default setting of your word processing package is
for all documents to be justified, in which case you would key in 'No'
to have a ragged right margin.

You can turn the justification facility on and off to make just a paragraph justified in your document. To practise this feature, load in the
file you created in Section 2.6, called EX2B, take your cursor to the
start of the paragraph you want justified and switch justification on by
following the procedure outlined above.

At the end of the paragraph, follow a similar procedure as above to
switch the justification off, but type 'No' alongside option 3.

5.5 View printing

If you are undecided which format, ragged or justified, would be more
effective, you can use the **View Document** facility to see the whole
of the page at a glance, exactly as it will be printed out. In general,
whenever you want to check the appearance on the printed page, e.g.
for CVs, sales literature, short letters, etc; it is sensible to view the
document before you print it out. To do this you need to press SHIFT
and F7, and then '6' to View Document.

You will see that the document appears rather small on screen. You
can change the size of the document on screen, by typing '1' for 100%
size, '2' for 200%, '3' for the full page view, or '4' for facing pages.

Press F7 again, which will take you back to the document on screen
should you wish to edit it before you print it.

5.6 Setting and altering left and right margins (and altering units of measurement) _____

As you become more proficient with the package you will want to use the flexibility of altering left and right margins after you have produced a document to improve its appearance for your particular purpose.

If you do not alter the margins in the way to be described, your document will use the margins which are already preset in the initial setup procedure of the package. These are called the default margins and are the margins always used by WordPerfect unless altered by the user. If you are feeling nervous about using WP facilities, you do not have to alter the margins at all!

To practise setting and re-setting margins retrieve the document you produced in Chapter 2 called EX2C.

To alter these margins, hold SHIFT and press F8. Press '1' to get the Line menu which you have already used for justification and line spacing. Press '7' for margins and type the measurement you wish your margins to be from the edges of the page, e.g. 2 inches for Left and 2 inches for Right and then F7 to exit from this menu.

The default is probably in inches, but it may be that you wish to work in centimetres. To do this, press SHIFT and F1 to access the **Setup** menu, which will look like the screen dump below.

```
Setup

        1 - Backup

        2 - Cursor Speed              30 cps

        3 - Display

        4 - Fast Save (unformatted)    No

        5 - Initial Settings

        6 - Keyboard Layout

        7 - Location of Auxiliary Files

        8 - Units of Measure




Selection: 0
```

Screen Dump 5.3

If you are using WordPerfect version 5.1 your Setup menu will vary slightly from screen dump 5.3. At this stage you have to select the Setup Environment menu by pressing '3'.

Select '8' (Units of Measure), type '1' for Display and Entry of Numbers, etc. and overtype the appropriate code, which is given on screen, i.e. 'c' for centimetres. Repeat the same process to access the Status Line Display, Setup: Units of Measure menu as shown below.

```
Setup: Units of Measure

       1 - Display and Entry of Numbers          c
             for Margins, Tabs, etc.

       2 - Status Line Display                    c


Legend:

       " = inches
       i = inches
       c = centimetres
       p = points
       u = 1200ths of an inch
       u = WordPerfect 4.2 Units (Lines/Columns)




Selection: 0
```

Screen Dump 5.4

Press F7 once to return to your current job.

If you are altering the margins on existing text, it may not alter its appearance on screen until you have used the Rewrite facility, which is described in the next section. If you are altering the margins at the start of a new blank file, you have done all you need to do to alter your margins.

There are certain conventions regarding margins for printed work. It is customary to have a wider left margin than right on business documents to allow for ease of reading when looking through a bound file. Suggested margins for a standard one-page A4 letter are 1.5 inches on the left and 1 inch on the right. Top and bottom margins are usually even and set at 1 inch from the top and bottom edge of the paper. This will give a pleasing white border to your work.

5.7 Altering top and bottom margins _____

You may wish to widen or narrow the white space at the top or bottom of your document and this is easily done as follows. It follows a similar procedure as for left and right margins.

Still working with document EX2C hold down SHIFT and press F8 to access the Format Menu. Select '2' to access the Page Menu and then '5' to alter the Top and Bottom Margins. Change these to measure 2.5 inches and press F7 twice to return to your document. Your 'Format: Page Menu' will look like the screen dump below.

```
Format: Page

    1 - Centre Page (top to bottom)      No

    2 - Force Odd/Even Page

    3 - Headers

    4 - Footers

    5 - Margins - Top                    2.5i
               Bottom                    2.5

    6 - New Page Number                  1
        (example: 3 or iii)

    7 - Page Numbering                   No page numbering

    8 - Paper Size                       8.27i x 11.69i
        Type                             Standard

    9 - Suppress (this page only)

Selection: 5
```

Screen Dump 5.5

The appearance of your text on screen will not alter, but you can see how it will look by using the Print Preview facility, (section 5.5). However, you may have noticed that your Status Line now reads 'Ln 2.5 inches' when the cursor is placed at the top of the document.

5.8 Rewrite _____

WordPerfect has a facility called **Rewrite** which you may not need to
encounter. However, you should be aware of it in case your text does
not alter its appearance on screen after you have altered its format, e.g.
changing left and right margins. It is likely that formatting changes
will take place automatically because this will be a default setting.

We recommend you keep the Rewrite facility permanently selected but
if you do not wish to do so, take your cursor from the top of the file,
and move it on down through all the text. As you do so, the screen
appearance alters to comply with the new formatting requirements.

However, the default setting on your computer probably means that
everything *will* alter on your screen, without you having to do this.
Should you need to switch the Rewrite facility on, follow this procedure if you have version 5.0. (For version 5.1 see the next paragraph.)
Press SHIFT and F1 to access the Setup menu, select '3' (Display),
press '1' (Automatically Format and Rewrite), and ensure 'Yes' is
written alongside this line. See screen dump 5.6 for how your menu
should appear.

```
Setup: Display

      1 - Automatically Format and Rewrite     Yes

      2 - Colours/Fonts/Attributes

      3 - Display Document Comments             Yes

      4 - Filename on the Status Line           Yes

      5 - Graphics Screen Type                  Text (no graphics)

      6 - Hard Return Display Character

      7 - Menu Letter Display                   BOLD

      8 - Side-by-side Columns Display          Yes

      9 - View Document in Black and White      No



Selection: 1
```

Screen Dump 5.6

For version 5.1 hold down SHIFT and press F1, then '2' to access the Display Menu and then '6' for the Setup: Edit-Screen Options menu and press '1' (Automatically Format and Rewrite), and ensure 'Yes' is written alongside this line.

5.9 Practice

The following invitation will provide you with practice in some of the display features described in this chapter.

1 Key in the following and save it as EX5D. You will need to centre the text and use double line spacing as described in sections 5.2 and 5.3.

<pre>
                    The Clerk and Governors

                              of

                    West Birtley High School

                        invite you to

                    the Annual Prizegiving

                 to be held at the School on

                    Saturday, 23rd October
</pre>

2 Set your top margin to 3 inches (see section 5.7) and, before printing this page, use the View printing facility to see how the invitation will look on the page.

5.10 Summary

In this chapter you have learnt how to

- overtype, insert and delete
- centre text
- use double line spacing
- justify text and alter margins
- view text alterations using Rewrite
- use View Document to see how printed documents will look

6 OPENING DOCUMENTS AND TEXT BLOCK OPERATIONS

In this chapter you will learn ways of moving, copying and deleting large areas of your work by first identifying the block of text concerned.

Key in the following exercise to practise the features of this Chapter and save it as EX6A.

```
LOUIS NAPOLEON

by Oscar Wilde


Eagle of Austerlitz! where were thy wings
When far away upon a barbarous strand,
In fight unequal, by an obscure hand,
Fell the last scion of thy brood of Kings!

Poor boy! thou shalt not flaunt thy cloak of red,
Or ride in state through Paris in the van
Of thy returning legions, but instead
Thy mother France, free and republican,

Shall on thy dead and crownless forehead place
The better laurels of a soldier's crown,
That not dishonoured should thy soul go down
To tell the mighty sire of thy race

That France hath kissed the mouth of Liberty,
And found it sweeter than his honied bees,
And that the giant wave democracy
Breaks on the shores where Kings lay couched at ease.
```

6.1 Marking text blocks

Before carrying out an editing procedure, such as copying a paragraph from one place in a document to another, WordPerfect provides a **Block** feature which enables you to highlight on the screen the exact parts you want copied. In other words a block of text is marked ready for an editing function to proceed.

This is done by moving the cursor onto the first character of the block of text to be marked. Using the text you have just keyed in practise this by taking your cursor to the start of the second verse 'Poor boy!'. With the cursor under the 'P' hold down ALT and press F4 (or F12). The words 'Block On' will flash in the bottom left hand corner of the screen. Move the cursor key down highlighting the whole of the second verse. You have completed blocking when the text you want has been highlighted, so you do not actually turn off 'block on'.

In version 5.1 you can use the mouse to block sections of text. Take the mouse pointer to the first character in the text to be blocked and hold down the left mouse button while you move the pointer down through the text. When the required text is highlighted on the screen, lift the button. The words 'Block On' will flash in the bottom left hand corner of the screen.

Having highlighted the text, the computer is now waiting for your instructions as to what you want it to do with this marked block. Go on to the next section to practise copying this block.

You could also practise emboldening the heading of the poem (EX6A) by using ALT and F4 (or F12), identifying the block of text with the cursor, and then pressing F6. Block mark Oscar Wilde's name and underline it by pressing F8.

Block marking is frequently used in WordPerfect for emboldening, underlining, italicising, etc., blocks of text which have already been keyed in.

6.2 Copying text blocks

Once you have marked the block of text in the way described above you can now copy it to another place in the document. With the block of text to be copied highlighted on the screen, press CTRL and F4 to display the **Move** menu, which will look like screen dump 6.1.

Select '1' for Block, press '2' to Copy.

```
LOUIS NAPOLEON

by Oscar Wilde

Eagle of Austerlitz! where were thy wings
When far away upon a barbarous strand,
In fight unequal, by an obscure hand,
Fell the last scion of thy brood of Kings!

Poor boy! thou shalt not flaunt thy cloak of red,
Or ride in state through Paris in the van
Of thy returning legions, but instead
Thy mother France, free and republican,

Shall on thy dead and crownless forehead place
The better laurels of a soldier's crown,
That not dishonoured should thy soul go down
To tell the mighty sire of thy race

That France hath kissed the mouth of Liberty,
And found it sweeter than his honied bees,
And that the giant wave democracy
Breaks on the shores where Kings lay couched at ease.

Move: 1 Block; 2 Tabular Column; 3 Rectangle: 0
```

Screen Dump 6.1

You will then be prompted on the screen to move your cursor to the place in the text where you wish a copy of this block to appear and press ENTER.

For practice purposes, move your cursor to the blank line underneath the third verse and press ENTER. Another copy of verse two will now appear between verses three and four. You will need to press the ENTER key again to insert a blank line between the third and copied second verse. (Apologies to Oscar Wilde for murdering his poetry!)

You might have thought the copied text would be placed on top of an existing passage, but you needn't have worried! WordPerfect simply moves everything down to make room for the newly-inserted words.

6.3 Deleting text blocks _____

This same procedure can be followed should you wish to delete a block of text, which you certainly will need to do if you are working on the poem exercise!

Move your cursor to the start of the copied second verse (ie. under the 'P' of 'Poor boy!' between verses three and four). Mark the block

(ALT and F4, move the cursor through the text to the end of the verse), and press the DEL key.

In version 5.1 the block to be deleted can be highlighted using the mouse and then pressing the DEL key.

Notice that the marked block of text has disappeared from the screen. Should you now change your mind and wish to retrieve this text, simply press F1 and it will reappear, then press '1' to Restore.

6.4 Moving text blocks

One of the most frequently used facilities of word processing is the ability to move chunks of text to gain a more satisfactory and coherent document. It will enable you to put random thoughts on screen and to assemble them in a more meaningful order after further consideration.

This is achieved by using the block marking feature once again. Practise moving a verse of the poem by moving the first verse to the end. Place your cursor under the 'E' of 'Eagle', hold down ALT and press F4, then move the cursor to the end of the first verse.

In version 5.1, you can again use the mouse to highlight the block of text to be moved.

Hold down CTRL and press F4 to access the Move menu. Select '1' for Block then choose '1' for Move. The screen prompt will instruct you to move the cursor to the position where you want your text to appear and press ENTER. Position your cursor at the end of the poem and press ENTER. The first verse is now the last.

6.5 Saving text blocks

It is very useful to be able to copy a block of text to a separate file, ready to be incorporated into a different piece of work. This is again done by following the block marking procedure.

Imagine you wanted to use the first verse as a quotation in another file. Again, mark the first verse of the poem. Hold down ALT and press F4, move the cursor to highlight this verse (version 5.1, you can again use the mouse to highlight the block of text to be moved), press

CTRL and F4 to get the Move menu, and choose '1' for the Block menu. Choose '4' to Append. A message on screen appears asking 'Append to'. Key in a new (or existing) filename, remembering to specify which disk drive you will require, e.g. A:EX6B. If you choose an existing file, the appended text will appear at the end of the file.

To reassure yourself of the success of this operation, load in EX6B and you will see the first verse displayed.

You could also practise emboldening the heading of the poem (EX6A) by using Block mark and then pressing F6.

6.6 Practice

If you would like further practice in Block marking then use this passage to practise the techniques outlined in this chapter. It may well be that you will have a passage of text of your own that you might prefer to work on. Any passage of text of at least three paragraphs will be adequate for this purpose. Save it as EX6C.

```
GARDENING CLUB NEWS

Spring is one of the best times to work on improving
the quality of your lawn, which may well have suffered
the ravages of frost, or children running around on it
when it was muddy.

Moss may have multiplied at a horrifying rate over the
winter months, and there may be bare patches in the
grass.

Weeds may seem to triumph  over healthy grass, and
although daisies look pretty in summer if you allow
them to flower, they spoil the healthy grass growth.
If left, they will eventually spread and kill off your
grass.
```

1 Swap around the last two paragraphs, to practise the moving text function.

2 Save the opening paragraph to a separate new file, as if you were going to re-use it.

3 Delete the last paragraph, and then use F1 to restore it.

4 Copy the top heading, to the bottom of the passage, as if it were the end of a gardening letter.

6.7 Summary

Blocking text hopefully holds no fears for you now. You should now understand that the block function is used to define passages of text prior to applying features like moving, copying, and deleting. This blocking feature will also be used when you format text in Chapter 8.

7 TABULATION

In Chapter 4, you were introduced to ways of displaying your text more effectively by altering your margins, centring, line spacing, justifying etc.

In this chapter, you will learn how to improve the appearance of your work by using **tab stops** to alter the alignment of sections of text, possibly in the form of columns, numbered inset paragraphs, or sub-paragraphs.

7.1 Use of tab key

You may have looked at your keyboard layout and identified the tab key. This is the key with two arrows on it and it enables you to align text at specific places on the page, where tab stops have been set by you.

If you wished to produce a piece of text like the section set out below, you would use tab stops to do so.

COUNTRY	CAPITAL	CONTINENT
France	Paris	Europe
Italy	Rome	Europe
USA	Washington DC	America
Thailand	Bangkok	Asia
Kenya	Nairobi	Africa
Australia	Canberra	Australia

First of all you need to have your ruler line displayed at the foot of the screen, so that you can see where the tabs are set. To do this, press CTRL and F3, and choose '1' for 'Windows'. Move your upward cursor key one line up and press ENTER. The ruler line will appear at the foot of the window and will display your tab stops, which at the moment are preset.

To use the tabulation facility, hold SHIFT and press F8 to access the
Format menu. Press '1' for the Line menu, which you have already
used for line spacing, justification and margins. Press '8' for the Tab
Set menu and check that your screen looks like the screen dump below.

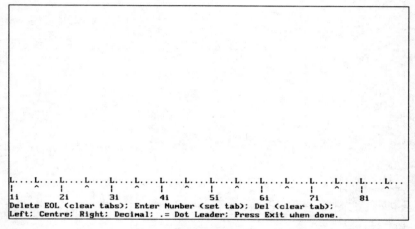

Screen Dump 7.1

You will notice that preset tabs are set at 0.5 inch intervals, i.e. the
default tab positions. Sometimes it can be useful to use these preset
tabs, where you only require tab stops at these points, but in most
cases, you will wish to set your own specific tab markers.

Key in the example given above, as a practice exercise in using the
tab facility, saving it as EX7A.

Before you start, you will want to clear the preset tabs illustrated in
screen dump 7.1 and set your own tabs. To do this, position your
cursor on the zero of the ruler line, and press the CTRL and END
keys to delete all the preset tabs to the end of the ruler line. Notice
that the tab markers have now disappeared from the ruler line.

Setting your own tab markers

Now you are ready to set your own tab markers. Appropriate settings for your tab markers would be at 1.5, 3 and 5 inches to display the three columns clearly. Move the cursor to the first required tab position (i.e. 1.5 inches) then press 'L' for left aligned tabs (which is the most commonly used form of alignment, whereby the inset text appears at the preset point, aligned at the left). Repeat this process at 3 and 5 inches and your ruler line should look like the one in the screen dump below.

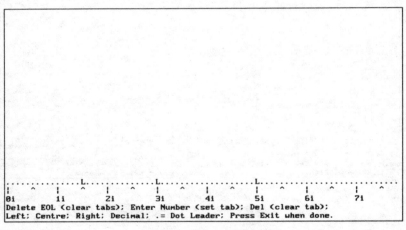

Screen Dump 7.2

Press F7 twice, and you will be returned to the screen ready to key in a passage.

Press the tab key at the start of each line, so that it is inset, and press the tab key once between each column of text, so that it looks like the example below.

COUNTRY	CAPITAL	CONTINENT
France	Paris	Europe
Italy	Rome	Europe

USA	Washington DC	America
Thailand	Bangkok	Asia
Kenya	Nairobi	Africa
Australia	Canberra	Australia

A slightly disconcerting feature of WordPerfect version 5.0 (but this does not happen with version 5.1) is that the ruler line gives measurements from the left edge of the page, and not from the preset margins. Take care, as the tab measurements given by you must be from the left edge of the *paper* and not the left margins, e.g. if you set a tab at 1 inch on the ruler line, and your margins were already set at 1 inch, the passage would not be indented in 1 inch from the margins, but would be flush with the left margin.

7.2 Moving tab stops

One of the excellent features of a word processing package is the ability to move tab stops quickly and easily, after you have keyed in a passage of text.

For example, in the above table, you could practise moving tabs by repeating the procedure for setting them. SHIFT and F8, '1' for Lines menu, '8' for Tab Set menu. Move the cursor to the first tab stop set at 1.5 inches, press DEL, and move the cursor to 1.75 inches and press 'L'. Move the other tab stops along 0.25 inches (e.g. to 3.25 inches and 5.25 inches) by repeating this procedure. The text will immediately move to its new position.

7.3 Decimal, right-aligned and centred tabs

With nearly all word processing packages, you have a choice of alignment for your tab stops. You can choose from left (which you used in sections 7.1 and 7.2), right aligned, centred or decimal tabs. The decimal tab is the one you are most likely to want to use when dealing with columns of figures.

Left	Centred	Decimal.	Right
Rome	Italy	£600.85	Sunny
Paris	France	£200.50	Cloudy

New York   USA   £1000.99   Misty

To practise using these special tab stops, do this tabulation and save
it under the name EX7B. Go into the Tab Set menu, as outlined in
section 7.1. Set a left-aligned tab by keying in 'L' at 1.5 inches, a
centred tab by keying in 'C' at 3 inches, a decimal tab at 4.5 inches
by keying in 'D', and a right-aligned tab at 6 inches by keying-in 'R'
at that point on the ruler.

With version 5.0 of WordPerfect, you can change the *position* of these
tab stops, but we would warn you that realigning tabs after the text
has been keyed in is not a straightforward procedure. However, the
following instructions explain how it is done.

You will have keyed in left aligned tab stops in your practice exercise
EX7A, now you are going to alter the left aligned tab stop for column
2 to a centred one. First you must re-set the tab stop on the ruler line
by using the DEL key to delete the 'L' tab stop and placing a 'C' in
the appropriate position. This centred tab should not be set on the
ruler line at the same position as the left aligned tab which you have
just deleted, as you must take into account the fact that the contents
of the column will appear further to the left on a centred tab, and
you will need to calculate the required position accordingly. Now take
your cursor to the top of the column to be re-aligned, i.e. the 'C' of
'CAPITAL' and press the BACKSPACE DEL key. Press the TAB key
to re-align the word 'CAPITAL' to a centred tab. You need to repeat
this process all the way down column 2.

This problem does not occur with version 5.1 of WordPerfect – once
the tab has been re-aligned on the ruler line and F7 pressed twice, the
column will automatically re-align.

7.4 First line indent for paragraphs _____

Paragraphs are frequently displayed with the first line indented five
spaces. This is an alternative way of displaying text, as opposed to
the current fashionable way of blocking text at the left margin.

   Just press the tab key at the first line of the paragraph, and
the text will go in 0.5 inches using the preset tab stop. Your paragraph
should look like this one.

7.5 Inset and hanging paragraphs _____

> To set the whole paragraph in by 0.5 inches from the
> left edge, press F4 and the paragraph will be inset 0.5
> inches from the left margin, *each* time you press the
> F4 key. In other words, two presses of the F4 key,
> will indent your work by 1 inch, and it would look
> like this paragraph.

Practise this by keying in the above paragraph, pressing F4 twice before
you start. Ensure you have cleared your screen after the tabulated task
you did in EX7B, so that you will be using the default tab settings.

> To inset 0.5 inches from left and right, hold SHIFT
> and F4, and the paragraph will be inset 0.5 inches
> from each side as in this paragraph giving these in-
> structions.

Each time you press SHIFT and F4 at the start of a passage of text, it
will indent to the next tab setting. If you are using preset tab stops, the
paragraph will be indented 1 inch by pressing SHIFT and F4 twice.

Alternatively, you could set a tab stop at the required indentation point,
e.g. 0.75 inches, if that is the point at which you wanted the paragraph
to be indented.

Hanging paragraphs look like this paragraph with the first line against
the margin, and subsequent lines inset 0.5 inches. It is an
alternative method of display.

Key in the hanging paragraph illustrated above, pressing F4 in front of
the second line and the paragraph will be indented 0.5 inches automatically until the cursor reaches a hard return (where you have pressed
the ENTER key).

Save the text from the various paragraph styles as EX7C.

7.6 Typing in left margin (margin release) _____

One of the main uses of typing in the margin is for numbering side
headings. To do this, hold down SHIFT and TAB keys, and the cursor

will move one tab stop to the left, each time you perform this action.

Try numbering the following paragraphs by pressing SHIFT and TAB once at the start of each line. Key in the relevant number and full stop, press the TAB key once and then key in the text. Repeat this procedure for each line. Save your text as EX7D.

```
1.        Stop at kerb.

2.        Look to the left.

3.        Look to the right.

4.        Look to the left.

5.        Listen all the time.

6.        Cross if it is all clear.
```

7.7 Centre page

A delightfully lazy way of centring a page like a cover sheet, where you want the text centred *down* the page, as well as across (quick reminder, F6 centres *across* the page), is to use the Centre Page menu.

First of all, load in the dinner menu you created and saved under the name EX5B.Then place your cursor at the top of the page, press SHIFT and F8 followed by '2' (Page), where you see the Format: Page menu illustrated below, then select '1' (Centre page: top to bottom) and say 'Yes'. Your screen will look like screen dump 7.3.

Finally press F7 twice to return to your document.

Nothing seems to have altered on the screen, but it will have done on the printout. You can gain assurance that the code has been inserted for centring the page by holding ALT and pressing F3 to reveal the codes, and you can then press it again to return your screen to normal. Alternatively, you can use the View Document facility to see how it would look when printed out.

```
Format: Page

    1 - Centre Page (top to bottom)      Yes

    2 - Force Odd/Even Page

    3 - Headers

    4 - Footers

    5 - Margins - Top                    1i
                  Bottom                 1i

    6 - New Page Number                  1
          (example: 3 or iii)

    7 - Page Numbering                   No page numbering

    8 - Paper Size                       8.27i x 11.69i
                  Type                   Standard

    9 - Suppress (this page only)

Selection: 0
```

Screen Dump 7.3

Try a simple notice, or perhaps an invitation, using the Centre Page menu, if you need more practice.

7.8 Practice

Key in the following text using margin release (section 7.6), hanging paragraphs (section 7.5), right-aligned tabs (section 7.3) and centre page (section 7.7).

CONTENTS

Page

Section 1   Prose passages for comment and
                 appreciation, including
                 principles of literary
                 analysis with appropriate
                 examples using contemporary
                 texts   v

Section 2   Poems and verse passages for
                 comment and appreciation,

```
                    including principles of
                    literary analysis of verse
                    with appropriate examples
                    of contemporary verse            xiii
```

Save your work as EX7E.

7.9 Summary _____

In this chapter you have learnt all you will need to know about tabulation. You have covered:

- clearing and setting tab stops
- decimal, right-aligned and centred tabs
- various paragraph indentation methods
- typing in the left margin
- centring text down the page

8 FORMATTING TEXT

In previous chapters you have started to appreciate the various ways a powerful word processing package, like WordPerfect, can enhance the appearance of your written work by varying the way it is displayed (double-line spacing, tabulation, centring, etc.).

In this chapter you will learn how to utilise features which actually alter the appearance of characters on the printed page. This is known as formatting text. Key words can be accentuated by underlining, printing in bold or italics, or made larger or smaller than the rest of the text. Some text will require different treatment from normal text, for example mathematical or scientific characters.

8.1 Underlining text

Probably the most common way you will wish to accentuate a piece of text is by underlining or underscoring. This is particularly appropriate for headings.

All you need do is press F8 and begin typing. From then on everything you key in will be printed out underlined although it will not be displayed on the screen. When you wish to return to ordinary, non-underlined text, simply press F8 again. This is another one of those toggle keys mentioned earlier.

Key in the following text, using underlining where indicated:

```
ACTION IN CASE OF FIRE

On discovering a fire:

Attempt to put the fire out if this seems possible,

but do not take any personal risk.

Inform the office manager of your action.
```

```
If it is not possible to extinguish the fire
yourself:

Sound the fire alarm

Call the fire brigade

Report the fire to the office manager
```

Keep this text displayed on screen, ready to practise emboldening in the next section, but save it as EX8A.

After creating or printing out work, you may decide that certain parts of it would stand out more if they were underlined. This is yet another occasion when your old friend block marking comes in.

Take your cursor to the first character of the text you want underlined, 'On discovering a fire:' and press ALT and F4, take the cursor along and highlight the text to be underlined, then press F8. The desired underlining will be shown on the printout.

Alternatively, you might have keyed-in text using the underlining feature, but subsequently decide you wish to remove it. To do this you need to take the cursor to the first character where the underlining begins and press the BACKSPACE DEL key.

8.2 Emboldening text

Another effective way of accentuating key words, especially in the body of the text, is to make their appearance thicker and darker than the rest. This is sometimes called **emboldening**. This effect is achieved in much the same way as underlining and can be activated before you key in text, or can be inserted afterwards.

If you think you would like something to be emboldened simply press F6, type in the text you wish to appear bold and press F6 again when you want to stop. Practise this feature by adding the following to the exercise you have keyed-in, emboldening as shown:

PROCEDURE ON HEARING THE ALARM

```
When the fire alarm sounds all persons will leave
the building via the east stairs and assemble in
the car park.


Do not re-enter the building until instructed to do
so.
```

Once again, should you decide upon viewing your work that it would look better if certain key words stood out against the others, emboldening can be easily added. You will need to define the block to be emboldened in the usual way (moving your cursor to the first character and pressing ALT and F4). Then press F6 to embolden the highlighted text.

Practise blocking text to be emboldened by using the fire notice again, and taking your cursor to the start of 'ACTION IN CASE OF FIRE', blocking it, and pressing F6.

Not surprisingly, to remove any instructions to embolden, the same procedure as for removing underlining is followed; take your cursor to the first character where the emboldening starts and press the BACKSPACE-DEL key.

8.3 Italics

Sometimes a small section of text is better displayed in *italics* to differentiate it from the main body of the text.

By convention, italics is used for words that need stressing, e.g. 'Children must *never* be allowed to play with matches'.

Practise putting text into italics, using the practice exercise EX8A, by doing the following:

Block the line beginning 'Do not re-enter the building' by taking your cursor to the start of the line, holding down ALT as you press F4, and moving it along to the end of the sentence to block the text.

Now hold down CTRL and press F8 to access the Attribute menu and select '2' (Appearance), then '4' which will put your existing blocked text into italics.

Italics needs a special mention here. This feature is not operated by toggle keys unlike underlining and emboldening. If you make the decision to use italics prior to keying in your text, you will need to follow the procedure below.

Hold CTRL and press F8, then choose '2' (Appearance), press '4' to switch on italics. Key in the required italicised text, and when you wish the appearance of your text to return to normal, hold CTRL and press F8 again but this time choose '3' (Normal). From now on your text will be displayed normally.

Practise this by adding the following text in italics to EX8A:

(Signed)   OFFICE MANAGER

8.4 Reveal codes

It can be really useful to see on screen what is actually happening when you use the editing/formatting functions. This is achieved by the use of the special WordPerfect feature called Reveal Codes or Hidden Codes. (This is also mentioned in section 3.9.) When you instruct the computer to alter the printed appearance of your document, codes are in fact placed in the document. All word processing packages place these instructions as coded commands and you can edit these commands in the same way as you can edit text, when you have activated the Reveal Codes screen.

Press ALT and F3 (or F11) to activate the Reveal Codes option.

Your screen should look like screen dump 8.1, with the top half of the screen displaying the text as normal, and the bottom half displaying the same text but with the coded commands clearly displayed.

A reverse video bar divides the screen in half and you will notice that the tab stops are marked by small white triangles. The start of the coded command appears in capital emboldened letters and the end of the coded command is in lower case emboldened letters, all commands being enclosed in square brackets.

As you move the cursor through the text, you will notice that where the cursor is in the top half of the screen, the same position is indicated in the bottom half by the character appearing emboldened. However,

```
Call the fire brigade

Report the fire to the office manager

PROCEDURE ON HEARING THE ALARM

When the fire alarm sounds all persons will leave the building
via the east stairs and assemble in the car park.

Do not re-enter the building until instructed to do so.

A:\EX8A                                      Doc 1 Pg 1 Ln 4i Pos 1i
                                         ]
[HRt]
[BOLD]PROCEDURE ON HEARING THE ALARM[bold][HRt]
[HRt]
When the fire alarm sounds all persons will leave the building[SRt]
via the east stairs and assemble in the car park.[HRt]
[HRt]
[ITALC]Do not re[-]enter the building until instructed to do so.[italc][HRt]
[HRt]
[ITALC]<Signed>  OFFICE MANAGER[italc][HRt]

Press Reveal Codes to restore screen
```

Screen Dump 8.1

when the cursor is on a space, it is not shown in the bottom half of the screen, and appears to be lost! Move your cursor onto a character, and you can see where you are.

Press ALT and F3 (or F11) again to restore the screen to normal, when you no longer need this facility. This is another example of a toggle switch.

8.5 Initial settings

You will have noticed that WordPerfect has default settings for format features such as line spacing, margins, tabs, etc. (see Chapters 5 and 7). Default means those values (single line spacing, tabs at half inch intervals, etc.) have been pre-set in the package and enable you to start keying-in text straightaway. WordPerfect calls them **Initial Settings.**

It may be that you wish to alter *permanently* the default settings on your version of WordPerfect because the type of work you do always calls for a specialised type of layout. To do this press SHIFT and F1 to enter the Setup menu, then '5' to display the Initial Settings menu, as shown in screen dump 8.2.

To give an example of how to alter the default settings, you are going

```
Setup: Initial Settings

     1 - Beep Options

     2 - Date Format                    1 3 4

     3 - Document Summary

     4 - Initial Codes

     5 - Repeat Value                   8

     6 - Table of Authorities

     7 - Print Options




Selection: 0
```

Screen Dump 8.2

to alter the Print Options. Press '7' to access Print Options. Your
screen should look like the screen dump below.

```
Setup: Print Options

     1 - Binding                        0i

     2 - Number of Copies               1

     3 - Graphics Quality               Medium

     4 - Text Quality                   High

     5   Banners                        No

     6   Form Number                    0




Selection: 0
```

Screen Dump 8.3

This can be useful if you normally require draft printing, or more than one printed copy. Enter your new default value requirements and press F7 to exit the Setup menu. These new values will now be a permanent feature of your version of WordPerfect and will be assumed every time you load up the package.

Remember that settings altered using the Format menu rather than the Setup menu will *override* the latter.

In WordPerfect version 5.1 the procedure for obtaining draft quality printing is different. Hold the SHIFT and press F7 then key in 't' for text quality and '2' for draft to alter the print setting.

8.6 Superscript and subscript characters

If the work you intend to produce contains mathematical or scientific formulae there is another formatting feature that will be useful for you to learn, the use of super- or subscript. This is where a character is placed either above or below the normal line of type, e.g. $400m^2$, CO_2 and, consequently, reduced in size.

To place a character above the normal line of type, position your cursor on the character before the one to be raised, press Ctrl and F8 to access the Font menu, then press '1' (Size) and then select 'Superscript'. All text from now on will be placed at this raised level, so to return to the normal position press Ctrl and F8 again then select '3' and 'Normal'.

The same procedure is followed to place characters below the normal line of type, subscript, but be sure to select Subscript from the Size menu of the Font menu.

Try typing 'H_2O' using the subscript feature and then '200°F' to practise superscript.

8.7 Flush right

It can be useful to align text **flush right**, particularly for something like an address or a personal letter. This facility means that all lines of text will finish with an *even* right margin, but the left margin will be *ragged*.

To do this, move the cursor to the start of the text to be aligned right, press ALT and F6, type the text you want and press ENTER.

Each time you press ENTER the align right command ends so you will have to press ALT and F6 again to make the second line of text right align. Try this out on the address below.

Flat 2A

Mansion House

London

EC5 4TN

8.8 Date key

WordPerfect supplies a DATE key and will automatically add the date to your work, by pressing SHIFT and F5, then typing '1' (Text), and pressing ENTER. (If you are using version 5.1 you do not need to press the ENTER key to carry out this command.) The current date will automatically appear. If you press ALT and F6, and then SHIFT and F5, the date will be right-aligned.

8.9 Overstrike

Another helpful feature of WordPerfect is **overstrike**. You can use this to produce characters of other languages (e.g. the Greek letter θ), or perhaps scientific symbols. This feature allows you to place two or more characters at the same place on a page, thus allowing the creation of specialised characters.

To achieve this, take your cursor to where you wish this specialised character to appear and press Shift and F8 to access the Format menu, then select '4' (Other) and '5' (Overstrike), and finally '1' (Create) to begin keying in the characters.

Now you can create the composite character by keying in each component sequentially. For example in the word 'Rhone', key in 'Rh' as normal followed by the menu sequence given above, then 'o' and '^' and press ENTER three times to ENTER the text to your document screen. This allows you to continue with ordinary keying in. You will notice, however, that only the last character keyed in under Create mode will be displayed on the screen. Thus, the word will appear as

'Rh^ne'. The hybrid character you have created will only reveal itself on the printed page.

8.10 Practice

This short piece of text requires you to embolden your heading (section 8.2), put key words in italics (section 8.3) and use superscript and subscript to display fractions correctly (section 8.6). Key in the text.

Changing Decimals to Fractions

Decimals can be turned into vulgar fractions very easily, for example the decimal number 0.7 becomes the fraction $^7/_{10}$ and 0.07 become $^7/_{100}$. Whole numbers, of course, remain unchanged, for example 3.3 becomes the fraction $3^3/_{10}$. Often, however, this direct translation will not produce fractions in their lowest terms and they must be reduced, for example 6.5 = $6^5/_{10}$ = $6^1/_2$.

The same system is applied no matter how many decimal places are used, for example 0.001 = $^1/_{1000}$ (one thousandth), 0.0001 = $^1/_{10000}$ (one ten thousandth) and even 0.00001 = $^1/_{100000}$ (one hundred thousandth)!

Save this complicated piece of text as EX8B and obtain a printout to check the effect.

8.11 Summary

In this chapter you have learnt about

- underlining
- emboldening
- using italics
- superscript and subscript
- flush right text
- using the date key
- using overstrike

You will find that underlining and emboldening, in particular, will be display features that you frequently use to make give impact to your work.

The other features are not used so frequently but super- and subscript and overstrike will be of particular use to you if you have specialist text to produce.

9 QUICK FUNCTIONS

9.1 Cursor movement

You should now be gaining confidence in using your word processing package, but it can be frustrating to have to move your cursor around on the screen, character by character. A list is given below of quick cursor movement commands to save you time and frustration. The best way of using these shortcuts, is to practise them on the following text which you can key in and save under the name EX9A.

```
As it spoke, I discerned, obscurely, a child's face looking
through the window, terror made me cruel; and, finding it
useless to attempt shaking the creature off, I pulled its
wrist on to the broken pane, and rubbed it to and fro till
the blood ran down and soaked the bedclothes: still it
wailed, 'Let me in!' and maintained its tenacious grip,
almost maddening me with fear.
```

Shortcut	*Keys to press*
End of line	Press END key.
Start of line	Press HOME key and left cursor key.
Move one word left or right	Hold CTRL and press left or right cursor key.
Move to start of file	Press HOME key TWICE and press upward cursor key.
Move to end of file	Press HOME key TWICE and press downward cursor key.
Move to top of page	Press PGUP key.
Move to bottom of page	Press PGDOWN key.
Move to top of screen	Press HOME key and up cursor key or – (minus) key.
Move to bottom of screen	Press HOME key and down cursor key or + (plus) key.

9.2 Search

There may be times when you want to search quickly through a long document and find a particular word or phrase either because you want to format it in some way (embolden or underline it, for example), or to modify it. The **Search** facility is used to achieve this. It would not be an appropriate method to use when you wish to delete or replace a word or phrase with an alternative throughout the document. In these circumstances, the search and replace facility described below should be used.

It is important that you specify exactly what you require the computer to search for. In other words, upper and lower case characters must be matched, i.e. instructing the computer to search for the word 'dogs' will not find 'Dogs' or 'DOGS'.

To search for any text, place your cursor at the start of the text you wish to search. Press F2 and type in the word or phrase you wish to find. Each time you press F2, your cursor will jump to the next occurrence of the word or phrase, and you can make any alterations as desired.

If you are at the end of a text file, you can press SHIFT and F2 to search *backwards* through the text.

An added dimension of the search facility that isn't immediately obvious is the ability to search for a formatting feature, such as underlining. Having found it you can then delete it, add an extra format like bold or italic, or change it to double underlining. To do this you press F2 and then F8 (the underlining key). The cursor will jump to the first instance in the document where underlining appears, you can then carry out your editing and press F2 again to proceed to the next piece of underlined text.

Practising the Search facility

To practise a very useful application of the Search facility on Word-Perfect, key in the following legal passage and save it as EX9B.

```
I, & of & hereby revoke all former Wills and testamentary
dispositions made by me and declare this to be my last
Will.
```

```
I appoint & (hereinafter called 'the executor') to be the
executor and trustee of this my Will.

The executor shall hold the proceeds of sale and all unsold
property and my ready money upon the following trusts:

a) to pay all my just debts and funeral and testamentary
expenses

b) to pay the residue absolutely to &
```

Now use the Search facility to locate the places the '&' occurs and replace it with an appropriate name. Obtain a printout, but it is not necessary to save the completed version of this document.

9.3 Search and replace

An added dimension to the search facility of WordPerfect, and one that you will use far more often, is **Search and Replace**. You can search for a whole word, part of a word, a number, punctuation mark, or coded commands such as the emboldening or underlining code we talked about in Chapter 8, and replace it with an alternative.

For example, it can be very useful when you become aware you have misspelt someone's surname throughout a document to be able to re-place it throughout with the correct spelling.

Another useful application of this facility is that it enables you to save time and effort in keying in complicated names or phrases. You can use abbreviations in place of the complicated text throughout the document, e.g. 'IT' instead of 'Information Technology'. When the document is complete, you can search for the abbreviation IT and replace it with the words Information Technology.

Yet another advantage in using the Search and Replace facility would be when you have used a particular format for sections of text (ie. emboldened or underlined certain words) but decide you no longer like this display feature. You can instruct the package to search for the code and replace it with DEL.

Practising Search and Replace

To practise this feature of WordPerfect key-in the following exercise
and save it under the filename EX9C.

In 1979 the EMS was set by the member states of the EEC. The
idea was to promote economic convergence in the EEC by
attempting to bring the economies of the EEC countries into
line with that of the most successful members, particularly
by reducing the rate of inflation.

The major innovation of the EMS was the introduction of a new
European currency, called the ECU. This is a weighted average
of the EMS currencies where weights are calculated according
to the relative importance of the individual currencies in
terms of key indicators such as national output and the
volume of trade with other EEC members. As the ECU is
calculated in the way described, obviously when new countries
join the EEC, the value of the ECU had to be recalculated.

The ECU performs the function of unit of account to the
exchange rate mechanism described below, and also provides a
currency which can circulate between central banks throughout
the EEC.

Now you decide to replace EEC with European Economic Community, EMS with European Monetary System and ECU with European
Currency Unit.

Move your cursor to the start of the passage, press ALT and F2, and
you will be prompted 'w/Confirm? (Y/N) N'. The default of No means
that all replacements will be made automatically. It is often useful to
have more control over what you are replacing, and to opt to confirm
'Y'.

You will be prompted now with an onscreen message of 'Srch:'. Key
in 'EEC', press F2 again, and you will be prompted 'Replace with:'
type in 'European Economic Community' and then press F2 again. If
you have opted to choose to confirm, you will have to key in 'Y' or
'N' until the search is completed.

Repeat this process for the replacements of EMS and ECU.

You can even search for the places in your text where you have pressed the space bar. This could be useful if you have inserted two spaces after a full stop, and wish to alter it to one space. You can also delete a word throughout a document, by keying in the offending word, and asking the package to replace it with delete, by pressing the DEL key at the replacement stage. An example of this could be where you have given someone a full courtesy title throughout a document, e.g. Mr John Smith, and you wish this to be altered to just John Smith.

9.4 Spellcheck and dictionary

Spellcheck is a very useful aid for proof-reading your work. For a hard disk system, you just press CTRL and F2 to start the spellcheck and '3' for Document. This will activate the spellcheck process and the first word recognised by WordPerfect's resident dictionary as being misspelt will be highlighted.

However, a note of warning if you are operating a twin disk drive system. You will need to be sure to *save* your work (press F10) and then remove your work disk before inserting the speller disk in drive B. Hold CTRL and press F2, choose '3' for Document.

The screen will now divide, giving your text with the highlighted misspelt word in the top half and a list of alternative spellings in the bottom half. (See screen dump 9.1.)

If any of these offered alternatives are suitable, press the appropriate alphabetic key written alongside the alternative. If none of the offered alternatives are suitable, then press '4' to edit the word. Key in your own alternative and press F7. If you wish to leave it unchanged, press '1' to skip in this instance, or press '2' to skip all occurrences of this word throughout the document.

If you are unsure how to spell any word, you can look it up in the resident dictionary. Start the Spellcheck procedure, but choose '5' to look up a word. Key in something remotely resembling what you want to spell and different alternatives will be offered. The shape of the word, however, has to be similar for WordPerfect to come up with the correctly spelt version.

```
The IMF believes that serious difficulties could be created
for the world-wide role of sterling when it enters the ERM of
the European Monetary System and recommends that entry should
be delayed for at least another year. It is the contrast
between the UK rate of inflation and that of fellow EEC
members which particularly worries the IMF economists.

IMF specialists forecast that this differential is unlikely to
narrow in the short-term, given the effect of the oil crisis
on the UK economy, although ironically they agree that early
entry into the ERM could have a beneficial effect on UK

===============================================================================

  A. elm              B. em               C. era
  D. ere              E. erg              F. erk
  G. ern              H. err              I. rem
  J. arm




Not Found: 1 Skip Once; 2 Skip; 3 Add; 4 Edit; 5 Look Up; 6 Ignore Numbers: 0
```

Screen Dump 9.1

9.5 Thesaurus _____

A thesaurus is a collection of words with similar meanings (i.e. synonyms). Therefore, when you are lost for words, WordPerfect's **thesaurus** can help you to find an alternative very quickly, e.g. if you
queried the word 'construct', 'assemble, build, erect, etc.' would all
be offered as alternatives.

Just place your cursor on the start of the word you feel you are unhappy
with, press ALT and F1 and a list of synonyms will appear. This
list will be split into nouns, adjectives, and even antonyms (opposite
meanings), from which you can choose your replacement.

Choose '1' (Replace Word) from the small menu at the foot of the
screen. You will then be prompted for the code letter of the word
you have chosen. They are shown in alphabetical order in the thesaurus. Key in the appropriate code and the replacement word will be
substituted in the text.

It is possible to use the thesaurus in greater depth than described above
by searching through lists of words. As you gain familiarity with the
package, you can experiment with this feature to view its full potential.

This is described in the next paragraph and shown in the screen dump below.

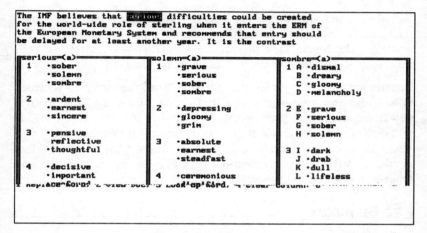

```
The IMF believes that [serious] difficulties could be created
for the world-wide role of sterling when it enters the ERM of
the European Monetary System and recommends that entry should
be delayed for at least another year. It is the contrast

serious=(a)              solemn=(a)              sombre=(a)
  1   •sober              1   •grave             1 A •dismal
      •solemn                 •serious             B •dreary
      •sombre                 •sober               C •gloomy
                              •sombre              D •melancholy
  2   •ardent
      •earnest            2   •depressing        2 E •grave
      •sincere                •gloomy              F •serious
                              •grim                G •sober
  3   •pensive                                     H •solemn
       reflective         3   •absolute
      •thoughtful             •earnest           3 I •dark
                              •steadfast           J •drab
  4   •decisive                                    K •dull
      •important          4   •ceremonious         L •lifeless
  1  Replace word  2  View Doc  3  Look up word  4  Clear Column  5
```

Screen Dump 9.2

By selecting the appropriate alphabetic key against one of the synonyms given, you will notice a second column appear on the screen containing a further list of synonyms for that word. Follow this procedure again, and a third column of synonyms is presented. This feature should ensure that you pick just the right word for your purpose.

9.6 Capitals switch

Experienced typists often find that they have left the CAPS LOCK on by mistake. It can be infuriating to get to the bottom of a paragraph and find that all the text is in capitals, when it should be in lower case.

WordPerfect has a most useful facility of switching text to lower case.

Key in the following text to practise the capitals switch facility, saving it under the name EX9D.

The ability to change text from all capitals to lower case
can be most helpful. TOUCH TYPISTS SOMETIMES FIND THEY HAVE
KEYED IN A WHOLE PARAGRAPH WITHOUT LOOKING AT THE SCREEN AND
FIND TO THEIR DISMAY IT IS ALL IN CAPITALS.

Just block the offending text in the usual way, but make sure you
include the full stop at the end of the preceding sentence, i.e. press
ALT and F4, move the cursor to the end of the text and press SHIFT
and F3. The Status Line displays '1 Uppercase: 2 Lowercase: O'.
Select '2' to put the text into lower case.

The reason for highlighting the full stop from the previous sentence
is to avoid any problems with initial capitalisation for the start of a
new sentence, because words like I'm and I'll are also recognised. If
you do not include the full stop, you will find that your sentences will
start with a lower case letter, instead of an initial capital. WordPerfect
is case sensitive if the punctuation mark is included and puts the first
letter in the sentence in capitals.

9.7 Summary

In this chapter you have learnt about a number of quick functions and
authoring facilities. These include

- searching for words or phrases
- searching and replacing
- using the spellcheck, thesaurus and dictionary
- using the capital switch facility

10 LONG DOCUMENTS

Up until now, although you have learned many features of WordPerfect, you have not covered any of the commands necessary for producing a multi-page document. These include where to start a new page, or how to number pages automatically and put chapter headings on every page. All these things enable you to create a very professional-looking piece of work.

It is suggested that you combine several existing files and make one long document to save you keying in a long piece of work. If you have used the suggested filenames, combine the exercises from Chapters 5.9 and save it under the name EX10A.

To achieve this, press F5 for your Directory, and press '1' to retrieve one of the chosen files. Move your cursor to the bottom of the first file, press F5 again, and press '1' to retrieve another of the chosen files. You will be prompted 'Retrieve into current document? (Y/N) N'. Key in 'Y' and the new text appears at the cursor position in the original document. Repeat this process with the other files.

Ensure it is at least three pages long, check by pressing the HOME key twice and then the down cursor to move straight to the bottom of the file. You will see from the status line how long the file is, i.e. 'Pg3', if it has three pages.

It helps to use the quick cursor movement of the HOME key, which, if pressed twice before pressing the downward cursor arrow key, takes you speedily to the end of your document.

10.1 Creating new pages

WordPerfect is preset to print out on standard A4-sized paper with 1 inch margins all the way round. Therefore when you are keying in your text it knows when you have filled-up one page and automatically moves on to the top of the next page. To show you where this page break falls, WordPerfect displays a dotted line across the page on the screen. You may have already encountered this while producing your own work and it is called a soft page break. This means that text can flow through this page break and on to the next page should you insert more text above it.

You may wish to override the preset page break because, for example, you are going to start a new topic, or you are near the bottom of a page and you do not want the automatic break to fall in the middle of a list. Note that you can only push the page break up the page. You cannot bring it lower down the page (unless you make the preset 1 inch bottom margin smaller – see chapter 5).

If you are keying in text and you want to start a new page simply press CTRL and ENTER. This time a line of equals signs (=) appears on the screen and you are ready to continue on the new page.

Take your cursor to the bottom of your practice text, hold down CTRL and press ENTER. A double dotted line will appear at that place in the text. You will notice that the status line changes and now displays the next page number. This type of page break is called a hard page break, and your screen will look like the one below.

```
Many people in business no longer communicate by telephone or
by posting a letter, but use fax machines. The fax machine
takes a document at one end of a telephone line, and
reproduces it at the receiver's end. Fax can even be used for
legal documents, drawings, sketches of fashion designs, as
well as for ordinary business correspondence.

==============================================================================

Using fax, the sender keeps a copy on paper of what has been
sent, and the receiver has the duplicate version to look at or
read, within seconds of it being sent.

                         TODAY'S MENU

                      Soup of the Day
                      Prawn Cocktail
                    Avocado Vinaigrette

                        Coq au Vin
                      Steak Tartare
                        Dover Sole

                  Sweets from the Trolley
A:\EX10A                                    Doc 1 Pg 2 Ln 11 Pos 11
```

Screen Dump 10.1

10.2 Breaking pages

If you notice subsequently that the automatic page break is in the wrong place, take your cursor to the first character of the text you wish to be displayed on the next page and press CTRL and ENTER. Do not forget you cannot make the page longer, only shorter, unless you alter the bottom margin, a procedure discussed in section 10.1.

You will notice that your Status Line menu now reads 'page 2' instead of 'page 1'.

Practise this on the long text.

10.3 Combining pages

With WordPerfect version 5.0, you will need to delete the soft page break that WordPerfect put in lower down the text and this is done by placing the cursor on the first letter of the text at the top of the page to be combined and pressing BACKSPACE DEL.

Alternatively, you will find that as you take your cursor on down through the document, it is 'rewritten', so that the soft page break disappears, although the hard page break is not removed by the rewrite feature.

With WordPerfect version 5.1, the soft page break will automatically be removed when you insert a hard page break.

This same procedure is also used if you wish to take out your hard page break. This is called **page combine**.

10.4 Page numbering

Page numbering is different with the two versions of WordPerfect. Follow the appropriately marked instructions for your version.

Having checked that you are happy with the way your document is split up on pages, by inserting hard page breaks and deleting soft ones if necessary, you are now ready to number the pages of this long document.

It is most common to start page numbering on the second page of a long document.

WordPerfect Version 5.0 _____

In this case take your cursor to the very top of the second page of the document and press SHIFT and F8, then select '2' (Page) and then '7' (Page Numbering).

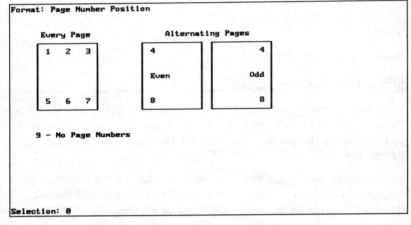

Screen Dump 10.2

A menu is displayed on the screen that asks you to make a selection about the Page Number position. For example, if you want your numbers to be displayed at the top centre of each page, select '2'. The Format Page menu reappears, press F7 or RETURN to go back to the document. Of course if you really do want your page numbering to start on the first page, you need to place the cursor at the very top of page one before carrying out the above operation.

If you wish to remove the page numbering, press SHIFT and F8, '2' (Page menu), '7' (Page Numbering), and then choose '9' (No Page Numbers), then press RETURN or F7 to go back to the document.

WordPerfect Version 5.1 _____

Take your cursor to the very top of the second page of the document and press SHIFT and F8, select '2' (Page) and then '6' (Page Numbering).

Choose '4' (Page Number Position). A menu is displayed on the screen that asks you to make a selection about the Page Number position, for example if you want your numbers to be displayed at the top centre of each page, select '2'. You are returned to your Format: Page Numbering menu, but you will see that 'Top Centre' is now displayed opposite the Page Number Position. Press F7 to return to the document.

Again, if you really do want your page numbering to start on the first page, you need to place the cursor at the very top of page one before carrying out the above operation.

If you wish to remove the page numbering, press SHIFT and F8, '2' (Page menu), choose '6' (Page Numbering), then '4' (Page Number Position) and then choose '9 (No Page Numbers). Then press RE-TURN or F7 to go back to the document.

10.5 Page headers

Yet a further sophistication to your long document would be to set up what is known as a **header**. A header is used to place the same information, a title with a page number included, for example, at the top of every page, or on every odd or every even page of your document.

Once again it is more common to place a header in a document from the second page onwards. (If you are going to include page numbering in your header you should not use the automatic page numbering procedure described above.) You place your cursor at the very top of the second page and then press SHIFT and F8 to access the Format menu, then select '2' (Page) and '3' (Headers). Your screen will look like screen dump 10.3.

WordPerfect allows you to put two headers on one page, this enables you to place a different header on odd and even pages (left aligned on even and right aligned on odd, for example).

A menu is now displayed at the status line and you will probably choose 'Header A' for your main header, by pressing '1' or 'A'. The Status Line menu changes and your screen will be like screen dump 10.4.

Press '2' (every page) at the Status Line menu at the bottom of the

```
Format: Page

    1 - Centre Page (top to bottom)      No

    2 - Force Odd/Even Page

    3 - Headers                          HA Every page

    4 - Footers

    5 - Margins - Top                    11
                  Bottom                 11

    6 - New Page Number                  2
        (example: 3 or iii)

    7 - Page Numbering                   No page numbering

    8 - Paper Size                       8.271 x 11.691
        Type                             Standard

    9 - Suppress (this page only)


1 Header A; 2 Header B: 0
```

Screen Dump 10.3

```
Format: Page

    1 - Centre Page (top to bottom)      No

    2 - Force Odd/Even Page

    3 - Headers                          HA Every page

    4 - Footers

    5 - Margins - Top                    11
                  Bottom                 11

    6 - New Page Number                  2
        (example: 3 or iii)

    7 - Page Numbering                   No page numbering

    8 - Paper Size                       8.271 x 11.691
        Type                             Standard

    9 - Suppress (this page only)


1 Discontinue; 2 Every Page; 3 Odd Pages; 4 Even Pages; 5 Edit: 0
```

Screen Dump 10.4

screen and you will now find you are presented with a normal-looking screen. Type in the title you wish to appear at the top of every page. If you want page numbers to form part of your header, ie 'Chapter 10 – page 2', then instead of actually keying in the number '2' hold down the CTRL key while you press the letter 'B' and you will see the following result:

Chapter 10 – page ^B. (This is what you will actually key in. Remember that CTRL is shown on screen by '^'.)

Incidentally you can centre (see section 4.2) or right-align (see section 7.6) this header if you do not want it displayed at the top left of your printed page. Do not bother to add any hard returns after this, as WordPerfect automatically inserts two line spaces after a header and before any text. Press F7 to exit and return to your document. You will not see the header displayed on the screen any more, but the coded command will activate the feature when you obtain a printout.

If you want reassurance that it will appear when you print the document, press ALT and F3 to Reveal Codes. Reassure yourself of the header's existence, and then press ALT and F3 again to make the codes disappear.

10.6 Page footers

Footers, as you might expect, work on exactly the same principle as headers but appear at the bottom of the printed page. You follow an identical procedure as the one described above, i.e. SHIFT and F8, '2' (Page) but then select '4' (Footer) instead.

Practise keying in a footer by typing your name as the footer text.

10.7 Page format suppress

If you have a reason for not wanting a preset header or footer (or any other page format feature) to appear on a particular page (there may be some full-page illustration you are going to insert subsequently, for example) you can use Suppress Page Format to override the command for this one page only.

Practise this feature on the third page of your text. Move your cursor to any position on page 3. Select SHIFT and F8, then '2' (page), then '9' (version 5.0) or '8' (version 5.1) (Suppress - this page only), and a Suppress Page Format menu is displayed. Choose the formats you want suppressed for this page only by selecting the appropriate option number and keying in 'Y' to suppress, and then press F7 twice to return to your document.

10.8 Centring page

All the facilities so far in this chapter have been about the body of the long document, but what about creating a really eye-catching front cover? For this you might want your text to appear centred vertically in the middle of a page, as well as horizontally, naturally. It is usually easier if you have a separate file for your front cover, to avoid complicated page numbering problems.

For practising this, key in your name and address, using any of the formatting features you might also like to try. Then return the cursor to the very top left hand corner of the page.

You start out in just the same way as you did above by pressing SHIFT and F8 followed by '2' (Page), then '1' (Centre page: top to bottom) and say 'Yes', finally press RETURN twice to return to your document. Again nothing seems altered on the screen, but it will be on the printout.

10.9 Control of hyphenation

When you have finally finished keying in your long document, don't sit back on your laurels yet, because there are still some other features that will help you to improve the presentation even further. The first of these is to set up automatic hyphenation, as the default is usually set for no hyphenation. This really makes a difference to the appearance of your printed work as long words are broken in an appropriate place thus avoiding an unnecessarily ragged right hand margin.

The two versions of WordPerfect are different here.

WordPerfect version 5.0
Take your cursor to the very beginning of your work and press SHIFT and F8, select '1' (Line) and then '1' (Hyphenation), then press '3' (Automatic) at the Status Line menu and finally F7 to return to your document. Now you must press the HOME key twice and the down

cursor to scroll through your work. Long words appearing at the end of lines are hyphenated as you go. Sometimes WordPerfect pauses to seek advice on where to hyphenate, in which case you need to move your cursor to where you wish the hyphen to appear, and then press ESC.

WordPerfect version 5.1 _____

Take your cursor to the very beginning of your work and press SHIFT and F8, select '1' (Line) and then '1' (Hyphenation), and press 'Y' for yes.

10.10 How to avoid 'widows' and 'orphans' _____

You still haven't quite finished with this piece of work, as there is yet another feature which will make a distinct improvement to your presentation skills. You may have found that with soft page breaks as described above, the first line of a paragraph may appear all by itself at the bottom of a page. This is called a **widow**. Alternatively the last line a paragraph may be left all by itself at the top of a new page, an **orphan**. These can be automatically avoided in this package.

Go to the very top of your long document and press SHIFT and F8, select '1' (Line) and then '9' (Widow/Orphan Protection), you now have the option of keying'in 'Y' if you want this feature, or 'N' if you do not. Finally return to the document by pressing F7.

10.11 Paragraph numbering _____

If this long document has numbered paragraphs WordPerfect allows you to set this up automatically too. Place your cursor at the beginning of the section where the numbered paragraphs are to appear and press SHIFT and F5 and select 5 (Paragraph Numbering) from the Status Line menu and press ENTER. It is suggested that you press the tab key afterwards, to take advantage of the preset 0.5 inch tabs to move the paragraph along to the right.

You need to repeat this process at the start of every paragraph to be numbered, and the number will automatically appear. The reason for having to repeat this process is, presumably, to give you full control over which paragraphs have to be numbered, and which are sub-paragraphs, not needing numbering. The paragraph number will increase by one each time you use this function.

One of the main attractions of this paragraph numbering, is that if you subsequently insert another numbered paragraph in the main body of your text, the numbers of the following paragraphs will automatically increase by one.

Practise this numbering on some consecutive paragraphs in your long file. If you have incorporated the poem, this would be an appropriate subject for this feature.

10.12 Summary

Your long document should now look most impressive. The document should now have the following features which have been covered in this chapter

- title page centred horizontally and vertically
- headers or footers included with page numbers
- hyphenated words to improve the ragged right margin
- page breaks put in appropriate places
- no widows or orphans
- automatically numbered paragraphs

11 USING MACROS

You may have found by now that you often seem to be repeating the key pressing procedure to carry out a WordPerfect command, or even typing the same piece of text over and over again, for example the ending to a letter. Help is at hand in the form of WordPerfect's **macro** capability.

A macro is the storing of any frequently used series of keystrokes in a special file, the contents of which can be activated by the pressing of a single key or a short filename.

In fact the advanced Macro feature of WordPerfect provides the flexibility of a powerful programming language. However, the simpler macros that are going to be described here are just a useful time-saving tool for word processing users.

11.1 Creating a macro

The type of operations which involve the repetitious pressing of a sequence of keystrokes are such things as the clearing and setting of tabs, putting text into italics, altering the line spacing of a document, justifying text, and altering margins to pre-set dimensions.

When you decide you want to store some frequently used keystrokes as a macro, you must first define it as such, in other words, give it a name that will be unique and help you to recall its use. After you have created your macro and come to store it, you will then be asked to name it by either keying in an eight-character maximum filename, or by simply holding down ALT while you press any one of the A-Z alphabetic keys. For example you might want to store a macro to access the Line and Tab Set menu and clear all the preset tab stops. You could name this either ALT and T or just 'Tabset'.

These macro files are stored like any others and can be copied or deleted in the same way.

Now practise creating your own macro for accessing the Line and Tab Set menu and clear all the preset tab stops, leaving the ruler line clear for you to set your own tab requirements, as mentioned in the previous paragraph.

Press CTRL and F10 and you will get a message 'Define macro:'. Press ALT and 't' and ENTER. Your screen message now says 'Description:' (no description is necessary for such a simple macro), press ENTER to continue. A 'Macro Def' message now flashes in the bottom left corner of the screen and you are ready to enter the sequential keystrokes required.

Now proceed by pressing the keystrokes you would normally choose to carry out this procedure for clearing tabs, i.e.: press SHIFT and F8, then '1' (Lines), and '8' (Tab set), now press the HOME and left cursor keys to return you to zero on the ruler line, then CTRL and END, and all the preset tab stops will be deleted.

Your macro is now defined and you need to stop defining it by pressing CTRL and F10 again.

You will now have stored a macro to carry out this function, and you are ready to test it out. The computer will have saved it and you can see it, if you wish, in your file directory, filed as ALTT.WPM.

Clear your screen, press ALT and 't' to test if the macro works and you will find yourself at the Ruler line, ready to set tabs.

Storing a short piece of text
Now try and store a frequently used short piece of text as a macro – a standard close to a letter, for example.

Repeat the procedure described above to define the macro: press CTRL and F10. At the 'Define macro' prompt, key in a filename (e.g. 'Letend'), just press ENTER at the 'Description:' prompt. Now you are ready to key in your text: 'Yours faithfully' (press ENTER) then key in your company name. Press ENTER 5 times to allow room for signature and then enter your own name. When you have finished press CTRL and F10 again, then F7 to clear your screen and 'N' in answer to the 'Save' prompt (it has already been saved when you pressed CTRL and F10 for the second time). Having created and saved this macro, test it out by following the procedure below.

11.2 Using a macro _____

How you precisely run your macro depends on how you stored it. If
you called it by an 8 character maximum filename then you press the
ALT and F10 keys and you will be prompted to enter the filename,
i.e.. 'Letend'. If on the other hand you named it with the ALT key
and 't', for example, you invoke it by simply holding down the ALT
key and pressing 't' and the automatic procedure will run. You can see
from this example that it is a good idea to keep your macro filenames
as short as possible.

As a very general rule we would advise you to use the ALT key naming
method for procedures like printing, merging, formatting, etc., calling
them P, M, F and so on, but for pieces of frequently used text such as
the close to a letter or a memo heading, use the filename method, as
this allows you to give it a meaningful label.

11.3 Changing and deleting macros _____

When you have tested your macro you may discover that it doesn't
run properly and then you will need to edit it.

You do this by again pressing CTRL and F10 (Macro Define) and
entering the same name, e.g. ALT and 't'. WordPerfect then gives
you the option of Replace (in which case the original macro definition
is deleted) or Edit.

You should only use edit if you wish to alter a text macro. To alter a
keystroke procedure macro (such as the tab clear one described earlier)
it is much simpler to use REPLACE and repeat the keystrokes rather
than attempt to edit them.

For making changes to a stored textual macro, e.g. the letter end stored
as 'Letend', carry out the following procedure. Hold down CTRL
and press F10, enter the filename 'Letend' and choose the option of
Edit. You can then choose '2' (Action), move your cursor within
the display box and alter 'faithfully' to 'sincerely'. When you have
finished editing press F7 repeatedly until you have cleared the screen

and the new version of the macro has been stored.

11.4 Summary

You have now learned how to store simple keystroke macros and execute them. Now think of some further frequently used procedures
and practise creating macros with them. As you become increasingly
familiar with WordPerfect, more and more obvious macros will come
to mind.

We strongly recommend that you spend some time mastering the macro
feature as it is so useful in dealing with the series of menus that
WordPerfect presents for many frequently used procedures. It can
save you a great deal of time.

12 MAIL MERGE

Imagine wanting to send out the same letter to lots of people, but at the same time wanting to make it appear individually typed. This is achieved relatively easily by the facility commonly known as **mail merge**.

In mail merge, there are always two files, one containing the standard letter which you wish them to receive, and the other file being your 'data' (most probably the names and addresses of your correspondents). The standard letter file is known as your **primary** file and the data file is usually your **secondary** file.

In the standard letter (primary file) you will put codes, which mark the point of insertion for the information contained in your data file (secondary file).

You are effectively *merging* the information from your data file into the standard letter file.

12.1 Creating mailing lists

If you need to do a mailshot, set up your list of names and addresses of people to whom you wish to write. It is usually easier to set up the secondary file (the data) before keying-in the standard letter to ensure that the fields are in the right place and the fieldnames are matched exactly.

First of all you must identify **fields** of information needed for each **record**. (See Figure 12.1 for an explanation of these two terms.)

Fieldnames are effectively the headings under which you store information, e.g. name, address, telephone number etc. Data is the information you will enter under those headings for each record, e.g. Mrs H Patel will be entered under the fieldname 'name' in the example exercise below.

A COMPLETED RECORD

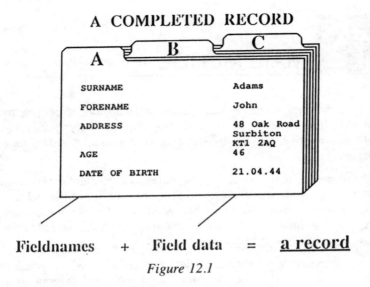

Fieldnames   +   Field data   =   <u>a record</u>

Figure 12.1

Before you can start keying actual information into the records in the secondary file, you must list these fieldnames in a very precise manner.

Key in the following text ensuring that your screen matches the one shown in screen dump 12.1 *exactly*.

To do this, hold CTRL and key in 'n', then press ENTER. It is necessary to embolden the fieldnames, which are 'name', 'address' and 'first', pressing ENTER after each fieldname to display them on separate lines as shown.

Now hold CTRL and key in 'n'. Press ENTER. Then hold CTRL and key in 'e', press ENTER. The letter 'e' marks the end of the entry for each record. Hold CTRL and press ENTER to create a pagebreak. WordPerfect uses page breaks to separate records.

You are now ready to key in data for your first record.

Remember that the ^ character means that you press the CTRL key at the same time as the alphabetic key (eg ^N is achieved by pressing CTRL and 'N'), and also that F6 (Bold key) must be pressed before and after each fieldname (e.g. 'F6nameF6'). You will also recall from

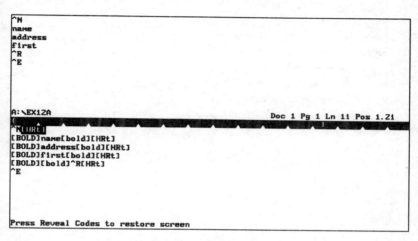

Screen Dump 12.1

Chapter 10 that the line of equals signs indicates a hard page break which is achieved by pressing CTRL and ENTER.

When you hold down CTRL and press R, you are telling WordPerfect that this is the end of data to be entered under this fieldname, e.g. Mrs H Patel^R means this is the total data to be entered under the fieldname 'name' for Mrs Patel's record.

We have provided you with three names and addresses to practise with. Key them in now exactly as shown, using the same line and page breaks:

```
Mrs H Patel^R
14 High Street
Guildford
Surrey^R
Hena^R
^E
CTRL and RETURN
Ms E Warriner^R
46 Lower Street
Midhurst
```

```
Sussex^R
Elizabeth^R
56^R
^E
CTRL and RETURN
Mr D Steinberg^R
75 High Street
Grimsby
Humberside^R
David^R
35^R
^E
CTRL and RETURN
```

Check your screen matches screen dump 12.2

```
Mrs H Patel^R
14 High Street
Surrey^R
Hena^R
^E
================================================================================
Ms E Warriner^R
46 Lower Street
Midhurst
Sussex^R
Elizabeth^R
56^R
^E
================================================================================
Mr D Steinberg^R
75 High Street
Grimsby
Humberside^R
David^R
35^R
^E
================================================================================
-> Srch:
(     ▲     ▲     ▲     ▲     ▲     ▲     ▲     ▲     )     ▲     ▲     ▲
```

Screen Dump 12.2

Save your work, giving it the filename EX12A.

12.2 Creating standard letters

You are now ready to key in the letter you want to send. Use the same field names as used in your secondary file, e.g. name, address, and firstname. It is essential that you key in the field names in the same way as you did in your secondary (data) file, i.e. matching capitals, etc. You do not have to make them bold in the standard letter though.

You need to ensure that ^F (CTRL and F) is displayed each side of the fieldname. Key in your letter as follows:

```
^Fname^F
^Faddress^F


Dear ^Ffirst^F

We would be delighted if you could come to a special showing
of the paintings of the little known Norwegian painter,
Brigid  Grunberg, which are being shown for the first time in
this country.

Light refreshments will be served from 11.30 am onwards and
we very much hope you can join us.

Yours sincerely



Gallery Owner
```

It should look like screen dump 12.3.

Remember to save your file, giving it the filename EX12B.

You can insert fieldnames in the body of the letter of course, just follow the principle of 'sandwiching' them between the merge codes (CTRL and F) and ensure there is a matching field in your data file.

If you are using verions 5.1 you can use the same method described above to create the secondary file, the one containing the names and addresses, but there is a different procedure for the primary file, the letter.

Clear your screen ready to key in the letter and hold down SHIFT

```
^Fname^F
^Faddress^F

Dear ^Ffirst^F

We would be delighted if you could come to a special showing
of the paintings of the little known painter, Brigid Grunberg,
which are being shown for the first time in this country.

Light refreshments will be served from 11.30 am onwards and we
very much hope you can join us.

Yours sincerely


Gallery Owner



A:\EX12B                                          Doc 1 Pg 1 Ln 11 Pos 11
```

Screen Dump 12.3

while pressing F9, then press '1' (Enter field). Key in the first field-name, which in this example is 'name' and press ENTER. Repeat this procedure for 'address' and 'first', placing them in the appropriate place within the letter, then complete your letter as above and save it as EX12B.

12.3 Printing mail merge files

This part is much easier! Just press CTRL and F9, select Merge at the Status Line menu, key in the name of the primary file, which will be 'EX12B', and press ENTER, if you have used our example, and then you will be prompted for the name of the secondary file. Key in 'EX12A' and press ENTER. Remember to insert the appropriate drive letter in front of filename to tell the computer where it can find the primary and secondary files, i.e. A:, B: or C:.

The screen will immediately display the merged letter as in screen dump 12.3a.

You can then print it in the normal way and save it as a separate file, if you so desire. However, it is not necessary to save it, as you can

```
Mrs H Patel
14 High Street
Surrey

Dear Hena

We would be delighted if you could come to a special showing
of the paintings of the little known painter, Brigid Grunberg,
which are being shown for the first time in this country.

Light refreshments will be served from 11.30 am onwards and we
very much hope you can join us.

Yours sincerely



Gallery Owner
==============================================================================
Ms E Warriner
46 Lower Street
Midhurst
Sussex
                                              Doc 1 Pg 2 Ln 1.331 Pos 11  .
```

Screen Dump 12.3a

always re-merge the two files, providing they are left intact. In fact, it is rather a waste of storage space to save this massive merged file, when you already have the two files in existence. If you do save it, use the filename EX12C.

Your final merged letter should look like the one below.

```
Mrs H Patel
14 High Street
Guildford
Surrey


Dear Hena

We would be delighted if you could come to a special
showing of the paintings of the little known Norwegian
painter, Brigid Grunberg, which are being shown for the first
time in this country.

Light refreshments will be served from 11.30 am onwards
```

and we very much hope you can join us.

Yours sincerely

Gallery Owner

12.4 Printing labels ————————————————

This is a relatively simple procedure. You can use your existing data file for this, but you will, of course, only be using the first two fields for the name and address, omitting the first name field.

Set up your primary file for the labels by keying in the fieldnames of name and address, ensuring that they are 'sandwiched' between CTRL and F.

```
^Fname^F
^Faddress^F
















A:\EX1ZD                                    Doc 1 Pg 1 Ln 0i Pos 11
(      ^       ^      )    ^      ^      ^      ^      ^      ^      ^
```

Screen Dump 12.4

You will now need to set up the label size. Press SHIFT and F8 to access Format menu, and '2' for Page. Press '5' for Margins, and key in '0' for top and bottom margins (*NB Do not use the letter 'O', but ensure you use the number '0' at the top of your keyboard, because computers do not recognize letters as numbers).*

Press '8' for Paper Size, then select '-'U for User Define.

```
Format: Paper Size

    1 - A4                         210mm  x   297mm

    2 - A4 Landscape               297mm  x   210mm

    3 - A3                         297mm  x   420mm

    4 - A3 Landscape               420mm  x   297mm

    5 - Label                      120mm  x   38,5mm

    6 - A5                         148mm  x   210mm

    7 - A5 Landscape               210mm  x   148mm

    8 - U.S Standard               8½" x 11" (use for 279.40mm continuous forms)

    9 - U.S Standard Landscape     11" x 8½"

    U - User Defined


Width: 41
```

Screen Dump 12.5

You will be prompted 'Width:'. Key in '4', and ENTER. At the 'Height:' prompt, key in '2' and ENTER.

Select '4' (Labels) to access the Format:Page menu. Check that the label measurements read '4i' and '2i' and '0' top and bottom margins. Your screen should look like screen dump 12.6.

Press F7 to exit and save this file calling it EX12D.

Now comes the easy part. Follow the standard merge routine of CTRL and F9, choose '1' (Merge), key in the primary filename 'EX12D' and press ENTER and then the secondary filename 'EX12A', pressing ENTER, and the merged file will appear on screen. You can now send this through to the printer in the usual way, by pressing SHIFT and F7.

```
Format: Page

   1 - Centre Page (top to bottom)      No

   2 - Force Odd/Even Page

   3 - Headers

   4 - Footers

   5 - Margins - Top                    01
                 Bottom                 01

   6 - New Page Number                  1
         (example: 3 or iii)

   7 - Page Numbering                   No page numbering

   8 - Paper Size                       41 x 21
             Type                       Labels

   9 - Suppress (this page only)

Selection: 0
```

Screen Dump 12.6

12.5 Summary

This chapter is quite a complicated one to get to grips with, but once you have mastered merging two files, you may well find it very useful. If ever you do need to send out a number of personalised standard letters, it is invaluable to be able to use this facility, to save the time and trouble of editing endless letters.

13 COLUMNS

Now you have seen how easy it is to produce really well presented work with WordPerfect you might want to write in columns like a newspaper article if you have a newsletter to produce. You may need more than two columns on the same page. This layout is called **Newspaper Style**.

An alternative column layout is **Parallel Columns** whereby you can have wordwrap *within* columns so that perhaps the third column has the most amount of text, like the example shown below.

Destination	Departure	Comments
Melbourne	13/12/90	Passenger in a wheelchair and needs special help.

Both these are simply achieved by using the **Text Column** feature.

13.1 Defining columns

Once column mode is set up WordPerfect treats each column rather in the same way it normally treats pages, in other words when the text you are keying in reaches the bottom of one column it flows on to the top of the next and so on. In fact you can even key in your document in normal format, which can be easier for screen proofreading, and then subsequently display it in newspaper style.

To practise column display it is suggested you use the following text and then set up the column display mode afterwards. Load in the file EX9C (from Chapter 9) and complete the article as shown below, i.e. starting at the paragraph 'The other important development'. Save this file, when completed, as EX13A.

In 1979 the European Monetary System was set by the member states of the European Economic Community.

The idea was to promote economic convergence in the European Economic Community by attempting to bring the economies of the European Economic Community countries into line with that of the most successful members, particularly by reducing the rate of inflation.

The major innovation of the European Monetary System was the introduction of a new European currency, called the European Currency Unit. This is a weighted average of the European Monetary System currencies where weights are calculated according to the relative importance of the individual currencies in terms of key indicators such as national output and the volume of trade with other European Economic Community members. As the European Currency Unit is calculated in the way described, obviously when new countries join the European Economic Community, the value of the European Currency Unit had to be recalculated.

The European Currency Unit performs the function of unit of account to the exchange rate mechanism described below, and also provides a currency which can circulate between central banks throughout the European Economic Community.

The other important development introduced by the European Monetary System was the exchange rate mechanism. This mechanism sets a band of value which allows each currency to move against any other European Monetary System currency by no more than a certain percentage. Once this limit is reached the countries concerned must act to prevent further upward or downward movement of their currency. This will mean intervention on the money markets to buy or sell the appropriate currencies. It may also mean a raising of interest rates for

that country whose currency is touching the bottom
of the exchange rate mechanism band.

The exchange rate mechanism was designed to provide
monetary stability within the European Economic
Community. The obvious disadvantage, however, is
that membership of the exchange rate mechanism
denies individual European Economic Community
governments the facility to adjust significantly
the value of their currency against that of their
major trading partners as a weapon to curb rising
inflation. Devaluation and Revaluation of member
currencies is only used as a last resort.

When you have finished keying-in this passage take your cursor to the
top of the document, ready to display it in columns.

Firstly you must define the type of column mode you wish to use.

To access Column Definition hold down ALT and press F7, then select
'4' (Column Definition) and your screen should look like the screen
dump below.

```
Text Column Definition

    1 - Type                        Newspaper

    2 - Number of Columns           2

    3 - Distance Between Columns

    4 - Margins

    Column    Left     Right    Column    Left    Right
     1:        1i       3.88i     13:
     2:        4.38i    7.27i     14:
     3:                           15:
     4:                           16:
     5:                           17:
     6:                           18:
     7:                           19:
     8:                           20:
     9:                           21:
    10:                           22:
    11:                           23:
    12:                           24:

Selection: 0
```

Screen Dump 13.1

For version 5.1 you will need to follow an alternative procedure. To access Columns hold down ALT and press F7, select '1' (Columns) and then select '3' (Define).

For both versions of WordPerfect, continue by selecting '1' (Type), which gives you a Status Line menu, then '1' (Newspaper).

Select '2' to access the number of columns section of the menu. You can have up to 24 columns, but three is probably sufficient for an A4 sheet of paper. Enter the number of columns you require and press ENTER.

You only need to access '4' (margins) if you wish to alter the column widths. WordPerfect assumes you want columns of equal width with the same margin between them and works out what they should be according to the number of columns you have entered (and of course the paper width, which is preset). You have the option to change any of these measurements, but you are advised to accept WordPerfect's suggestions, at least when you are a beginner. Do this by pressing F7 twice to continue and exit this Column Definition menu.

13.2 Using column mode

Now that the type of Column mode you wish to use has been defined you are ready to turn on Columns. To do this you move the cursor to the place where you wish your newspaper-style columns to begin, i.e. at the top of EX13A, and press ALT and F7 again. Now select '3' (Column On/Off).

For version 5.1 press ALT and F7, type '1' (Columns) and then '1' (On).

As you are placing pre-entered text in Column mode you use the Rewrite facility and move your cursor down through the text. You will find that immediately you start to move the cursor down, all the subsequent text is displayed in the column format that you have selected.

Like page breaks you can also determine where you want a column to break by inserting hard page breaks at the appropriate place (CTRL and ENTER).

If you have set up column display before keying in, anything you type from now on will appear in column format.

13.3 Leaving column mode

When you have finished keying in your newspaper-style text, or when your cursor is at the bottom of the text you want to appear in this style, you must execute the Turn Off Columns command. To do this press ALT and F7 to access the Maths/Columns menu, select '3' (Column On/Off).

For version 5.1, press ALT and F7, select '1' (Columns) and then '2' (Off).

Any text that follows will be displayed in the normal format.

However, should you decide against the whole idea of columns, you can instruct WordPerfect to display your document in the normal page format. To do this place your cursor on the first character to appear in column mode and press BACKSPACE DEL twice. Your text will return to normal format.

13.4 Editing columns

If you want to edit while in Column mode you will find that the up and down arrow keys and the PgUp and PgDn keys move up and down the whole page, whereas the right and left arrow keys and the HOME key move within the column. The delete keys treat a column in the same way they treat a page in Normal mode.

If you want to move your cursor from column to column to carry out editing, press CTRL and HOME together. A 'Go to' message at the Status Line will appear and you move the cursor key right or left, in other words in whichever direction you wish to go.

Should you subsequently decide that part of your column mode text would look better in normal page mode, take your cursor to the first character of the column you wish to display in normal format. Press ALT and F7 to access the Maths/Column Status Line menu and select '3' (Column On/Off) so that you have effectively *switched off* from this point on. You will need to pass your cursor through the remainder of the text you now wish displayed in normal format.

13.5 Parallel columns _____

To create parallel or side by side columns, you follow the same procedure as outlined above regarding Column definition, except that when
you are specifying the type of column you require, you choose '2'
(Parallel) at the Status Line menu. Follow the other steps for Column
definition.

Unlike Newspaper Style, however, it is recommended that you set up
Parallel Columns before you start keying-in.

Key in the text you require to be in column 1, and then hold down
CTRL and press ENTER. The cursor will then jump to the start of the
next column, and wordwrap will take place within that column. When
you have finished with column 2, press CTRL and ENTER again and
you will be at the head of column 3 (if you have chosen 3 column
format).

Practise this now on the text below. Key in 'Destination' and hold
down CTRL and press ENTER to move to the top of column 2. Now
key-in 'Departure' and press CTRL and ENTER to move to the top
of column 3. When you have keyed in 'Comments' you should press
ENTER twice in the normal way and you will be back in column 1
ready to key in 'Melbourne'. Hold down CTRL and press ENTER to
move to column 2 and key in the date given, then CTRL and ENTER
again to move to column 3. Type in the text under comments for
'Melbourne' but do not press ENTER until you have finished. Your
cursor will then be returned to column 1 ready for keying in details
about 'Auckland'. Follow this procedure to complete the table, saving
your work as EX13B.

Destination	Departure	Comments
Melbourne	13/12/90	Passenger in a wheelchair and needs special help.
Auckland	15/01/91	12 vegetarian meals

```
                              required - no fish

   Honolulu      02/02/91     1 diabetic passenger
                              - special low-sugar
                              diet required
```

If you regret where you have broken your columns, just place your cursor on the first character, perhaps the start of the second column, press BACKSPACE DELETE and it will be amalgamated with column 1. Wherever you press CTRL and ENTER is where the column will break.

13.6 Practice in parallel columns _____

Practise parallel columns using the exercise at the start of the chapter. Set tab stops at 1.5″, 3″, 4.5″. Tab to first tab stop. Key in 'Destination', press RETURN twice. Key in Melbourne and press CTRL and ENTER. Key in the Departure column in the same way, pressing CTRL and ENTER at the foot of column 2. Your cursor will now be at the top of column 3 and you will notice the text will wordwrap within the column.

To enhance the appearance of your work even further, you could place a bold, centred heading across the top of the page and then start your column display beneath. This can look very professional. To practise this in EX13A place a bold, centred heading at the top of your article: 'The European Monetary System'.

You can also experiment with parallel columns, which is a useful feature and is easy to use, once you have mastered using the Column menu.

Even if you haven't actually got an assignment of this type to produce at the moment, you might like to call up an old document and practise putting the text into columns. You could then also experiment with a different number of columns across the page to see which effect you prefer. Also practise breaking a column at a specific place to leave enough room to place a photograph or graphic in the empty space.

13.7 Summary

In this chapter you have learned how to display your work in two or more columns across a page which is generally appropriate for newspaper articles or a newsletter.

14 ADVANCED WORDPERFECT

A number of fairly advanced functions are grouped together in this chapter but there are many more you can use if you look through the WordPerfect manual. By the time you have worked through this book, you will be familiar with WordPerfect and its features and will feel confident enough to look up advanced features as you require them.

14.1 Using the column total function

Quite often you will need to key in a column of figures, and it is useful to be able to add them up without having to resort to the use of a calculator. This is quite easy to do by following this procedure. Practise by keying in the following table, saving it as EX14A.

	August	September
Credit Sales	45,789	56,345
Cash Sales	30,543	40,250

Move your cursor to where you wish to start using the maths function, i.e at the start of where the figures are keyed in. You must set tab stops (obviously they will need to be decimal tabs since you are dealing with figures) for the columns you are going to use, say at 3 and 5 inches.

Access the Maths/Columns menu by pressing ALT and F7. Turn on Maths by typing '1'. Your screen will look like screen dump 14.1.

Key in a plus sign (+) at the tab stop for the August column as this is where you would wish your answer to be displayed. You must use the plus sign located above the equals sign in the top row of your keyboard, as WordPerfect does not recognise the plus sign located on the number pad.

Press ALT and F7. Type '2' to Calculate. Using the Tab key, move to the second column and repeat the procedure (do not forget the + sign) and then press ALT and F7, followed by 1 to turn Maths off. In both

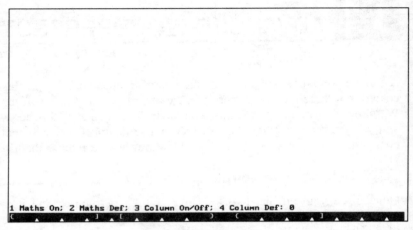

1 Maths On; 2 Maths Def; 3 Column On/Off; 4 Column Def: 0

Screen Dump 14.1

cases, the answer will appear at the foot of the column.

Should you alter a figure in your column, you will need to recalculate the total.

WordPerfect will only total a column of figures. It will not total the figures if they are displayed in rows, and you want the answer to appear in the same row.

14.2 Locking documents using a password ———

This can be useful if you have confidential work which you alone wish to access, or if you want to limit access to those people who know the password. A password adds extra security to a file, and once this is given to a file, no one can look at the file or print it until the password is given. WordPerfect allows you to use punctuation, spaces and more than one word in composing your password. However, take care not to make things too complicated for yourself.

Make sure that no one can see the password you are keying in. To help with this WordPerfect keeps the screen blank at the point of entry of the password, and you have to key it in twice.

Load in a file in the usual way. It is probably best at this stage to use one which does not matter should you forget the password and therefore lose the file. Press CTRL and F5 and your screen will look like the screen dump below.

```
The IMF believes        inflation and           UK and in other
that serious            that of fellow          EEC countries -
difficulties            EEC members which       namely the
could be created        particularly            inclusion of
for the world-          worries the IMF         mortgage interest
wide role of            economists.             repayments as a
sterling when it                                factor in the UK.
enters the ERM of       IMF specialists
the European            forecast that           Most experts -
Monetary System         this differential       both in the UK
and recommends          is unlikely to          and in other EEC
that entry should       narrow in the           countries - agree
be delayed for at       short-term, given       that the current
least another           the effect of the       exchange rate of
year. It is the         oil crisis on the       sterling against
contrast between        UK economy,             other European
the UK rate of          although                Monetary System
inflation and           ironically they         currencies is
that of fellow          agree that early        unsustainably
EEC members which       entry into the          high. One factor
particularly            ERM could have a        particularly
worries the IMF         beneficial effect       affecting this is
economists.             on UK inflation.        the role of
1 DOS Text; 2 Password; 3 Save Generic; 4 Save WP 4.2; 5 Comment: 0
```

Screen Dump 14.2

Select '2' (Password) and '1' (Add).

Key in your password and then key it in again when asked to do so. Save your file again, and clear your screen in the usual way.

When you try to retrieve it (SHIFT and F10) you will find that you have to enter the password. Once you have entered it, the file will appear.

It is easy to remove the password if you *know* it, by pressing CTRL and F5, select '2' (Password), and '2' (Remove). You are the only person who can do this, because it has to be done *within* the locked file, i.e. when it is loaded on screen. Then save your file again as the unlocked version.

If you have forgotten the password, there is no way to unlock it!

117

14.3 Sorting lists

WordPerfect has an incredibly powerful sorting facility, enabling you to use up to nine different criteria. It is highly unlikely you will ever need to use more than three. Do not be put off by the apparent complexity of the menu when, in fact, it operates very simply.

Key in the following list, setting suitable tab stops:

Name	Town	County	Age
Peter Smith	Halifax	Yorks	46
Jim Ward	Guildford	Surrey	34
Frances Alexander	Plymouth	Devon	29
Bronwen Thomas	Rhayader	Powys	65
Annabelle Lee	Kings Lynn	Norfolk	16

Assume you want to sort your list on the screen as a block of text, line-by-line, i.e. record-by-record.

First of all mark it as a block. Move your cursor to the start of the list, i.e. to the letter 'P' of 'Peter' and then block the text, by using Alt and F4. Take the cursor down through the list, highlighting all the lines to be included in the sort. Be sure, however, not to include your column headings (the field names) in the identified block of text or they will be resorted along with the records.

WordPerfect 5.1 users, of course, have the use of the mouse to highlight the block of text containing the records.

Hold down CTRL and press F9 to access the Sort by Line menu and the split-screen shown in screen dump 14.3 will appear.

It may appear rather bewildering at first, but basically it is offering you the facility of sorting your lines of text into a different order using nine criteria (Keys 1 to 9) in order of priority. You are unlikely to use more than three levels of priority in your sorting, but they might be useful if you had a large number of records with the same surname, for example.

For the simple example here, you are only going to use one criterion, and thus only one priority, alphabetic order of surname, i.e. sorting on

```
Peter Smith          Halifax      Yorks     46
Jim Ward             Guildford    Surrey    34
Frances Alexander    Plymouth     Devon     29
Bronwen Thomas       Rhayader     Powys     65
Annabelle Lee        Kings Lyn    Norfolk   16




                                        Doc 2 Pg 1 Ln 1" Pos 1"
[                                                              ]
------------------------------- Sort by Line -------------------------------
Key Typ Field Word        Key Typ Field Word        Key Typ Field Word
 1   a     1     2         2                         3
 4                         5                         6
 7                         8                         9
Select

Action                    Direction                 Type
Sort                      Ascending                 Line sort

1 Perform Action; 2 View; 3 Keys; 4 Select; 5 Action; 6 Order; 7 Type: 0
```

Screen Dump 14.3

the second word in the first column.

With the Sort by Line menu displayed, press '3' (Keys) and you are now in a position to choose the criteria for your first sort priority under Key 1. You will need to state whether the data in the field is alphanumeric or numeric ('a' or 'n'). Using the exercise, the first three columns will be alphanumeric and the last column will be numeric.

You now select the fields on which to sort (i.e. column 1 or 2, 3 or 4 in our example). In this case it is going to be column 1, the column where 'Name' appears. Enter '1' under Field. The fieldname Name in our records gives the surname as the second word in the field, so enter '2' under 'Word'. Press F7 when you have completed this procedure.

You are offered a choice for the sort order, ascending (A – Z or numeric 1 upwards) or descending (Z – A or starting at highest number down-wards). Select the order you want by pressing '6' (Order) at the Sort by Line menu, and then either '1' (Ascending) or '2' (Descending). You will then be returned to the Sort by Line menu.

Check that you have filled in the Sort by Line menu giving the correct criteria and priorities. If you are using our example your screen should

Name	Town	County	Age
Frances Alexander	Plymouth	Devon	29
Annabelle Lee	Kings Lyn	Norfolk	16
Peter Smith	Halifax	Yorks	46
Bronwen Thomas	Rhayader	Powys	65
Jim Ward	Guildford	Surrey	34

A:\EX14B   Doc 1 Pg 1 Ln 1.33" Pos 1"

Screen Dump 14.4

look like screendump 14.4.

Now press '1' (Perform Action) and the resorting of your records into alphabetic order of surname will have taken place. Press F7 to exit and return to your normal keying-in screen.

Your records should now be displayed on the screen in the order shown in the screendump below.

Print this out if you want a copy of the file in this order.

Practise this procedure by sorting your records into descending age order. Define your block as before and then hold down CTRL while pressing F9 to access the Sort by Line menu. Choose 3 (Keys) to enter the new sorting criteria, remembering this time you will have to key in 'n' (numeric) under 'type', '4' under 'Field' , and '1' under 'Word' and press F7. Now press 6 (Order) and choose Descending. Press F7 and then '1' (Perform Action) to carry out the sort.

Try printing out the sorted file again.

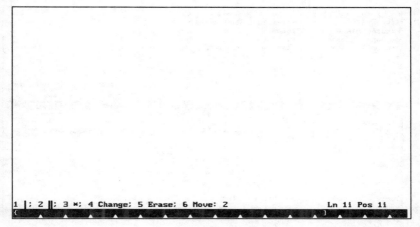

Screen Dump 14.5

14.4 Repeat key

The ESC key will repeat a single keystroke. For example if you want a line of 15 asterisks, all you have to do is press ESC, key in the number of times you want something repeated, e.g. '15', type '*' and 15 asterisks will appear. This is probably not something you will use frequently, but you may find it of some use in display work.

Another use of it is a double line, achieved by using '=' sign, e.g. ESC, key in '20', type '=', and a double line of 20 characters will appear.

14.5 Drawing lines and boxes

Designing forms is much easier if you can use a line or box drawing facility within your word processing package.

To draw a line, place the cursor where you want to start your line. Press CTRL and F3 (Screen) and select '2' (Line Draw). You can choose between a single (1) or a double line (2); press '2' in this instance.

```
Peter Smith          Halifax      Yorks     46
Jim Ward             Guildford    Surrey    34
Frances Alexander    Plymouth     Devon     29
Bronwen Thomas       Rhayader     Powys     65
Annabelle Lee        Kings Lyn    Norfolk   16




                                          Doc 2 Pg 1 Ln 1" Pos 1"
[              ▲              ▲              ▲           ]
------------------------------ Sort by Line ------------------------------

Key Typ Field Word    Key Typ Field Word    Key Typ Field Word
 1   a    1     1      2                     3
 4                     5                     6
 7                     8                     9
Select

Action                Direction             Type
Sort                  Ascending             Line sort

1 Perform Action; 2 View; 3 Keys; 4 Select; 5 Action; 6 Order; 7 Type: 0
```

Screen Dump 14.6

There are two ways of achieving this. You can now either move the cursor to where you want the line to end, or press ESC and enter the number of lines or spaces you wish the line to extend and then press the cursor key in the direction you wish the line to go. Press F7 when you have completed the line.

If you are drawing a box, you can draw the whole of the box using the cursor keys, when you are at the Line Draw menu. If you overshoot the corners, press '5' to erase, and move the cursor along the offending portion of the line. Press F7 when it is complete.

If you wish to insert text within your box, you will have to use the Overtype mode, which is achieved by pressing INS. This will enable you to type within the boundaries of the box.

You can also draw boxes *around* your text, e.g. for a cover page – this can be another useful display feature.

If you want to move the cursor without drawing a line when you are in the Line Draw menu, type '6', and this will enable you to place the cursor in another area of the screen to draw another line, once you have reselected a single or double line (1 or 2).

14.6 Summary

This chapter has introduced you to several advanced features which we are sure you will find useful. WordPerfect has more advanced features which have not been covered in this book as it is intended for the beginner and intermediate standard user. You will be able to find these out by looking through your manual.

15 PRACTICE EXERCISES

The series of exercises in this chapter will give you extra practice in using the features of WordPerfect. They are graded in order of difficulty, but provide revision in basic functions as well.

If you are using a hard disk system it is suggested you create a new directory for storing the exercises (Section 4.5).

Chapter references are given so that you can look back in the book to refresh your memory.

15.1 Exercise 1

Instructions for exercise

1 Key in the following piece and save it as EX15A. Print out a copy of this document using the printing current document facility (Section 3.1).

2 Use the block marking facility (Section 6.1) to underline the main heading of this passage (Section 8.1), centre (Section 5.2) and embolden it (Section 8.2).

3 Use Spellcheck on this document to check for any keying in errors (Section 9.4).

4 Use the block marking facility (Section 6.1) to block the last paragraph and move it so that it is the third paragraph.

5 Save the document under the new filename EX51B, and print out a revised copy.

Paul Cezanne (1839.1906)

Cezanne was born in Aix-en-Provence. His father was a
wealthy local businessman. He studied law at the
College Bourbon where he became a close friend of
Emile Zola. In fact many believed, including Cezanne
himself, that he was the model for the character of
Claude Lantier in Zola's L'Oeuvre. This displeased
Cezanne greatly and put an end to the friendship.

In 1862 he went to Paris where he met Pisarro, with
whom he worked for many years. Together they
developed an impressionist technique for landscapes.
Although Cezanne also produced some rather violent
and erotic pictures during this time.

Over the years Cezanne grew away from the
impressionist technique and became more classicist in
his use of colour as the ultimate expression of the
underlying forms of visible objects. He believed that
the artist must look for the cone, the sphere and the
cylinder in nature. Ideas of this type have given him a
claim to be an earlier exponent of cubism.

When, in 1886 Paul Cezanne's father died, he inherited
sufficient wealth to return to Provence and live there
in comparative seclusion. During these last years of
his life he returned to painting landscapes and still-
life with intensely careful analysis - so much so that
many works were never finished. He produced few
portraits, but those he did required endless sittings.

His works of art are displayed all over the world -
notably in London, New York and Paris.

Your document should look like the example below.

Paul Cezanne (1839.1906)

Cezanne was born in Aix-en-Provence. His father was a
wealthy local businessman. He studied law at the College
Bourbon where he became a close friend of Emile Zola. In
fact many believed, including Cezanne himself, that he was
the model for the character of Claude Lantier in Zola's
L'Oeuvre. This displeased Cezanne greatly and put an end to
the friendship.

In 1862 he went to Paris where he met Pisarro, with whom
he worked for many years. Together they developed an
impressionist technique for landscapes. Although Cezanne
also produced some rather violent and erotic pictures during
this time.

Over the years Cezanne grew away from the impressionist
technique and became more classicist in his use of colour as
the ultimate expression of the underlying forms of visible
objects. He believed that the artist must look for the cone,
the sphere and the cylinder in nature. Ideas of this type
have given him a claim to be an earlier exponent of cubism.

His works of art are displayed all over the world - notably
in Amsterdam, Basle, Berlin, Chicago, Essen, Hamburg,
Helsinki, London, Los Angeles, Munich, New York, Ottawa,
Paris, Prague, Stockholm and Zurich.

When, in 1886 Paul Cezanne's father died, he inherited
sufficient wealth to return to Provence and live there in
comparative seclusion. During these last years of his life he
returned to painting landscapes and still-life with intensely
careful analysis - so much so that many works were never
finished. He produced few portraits, but those he did
required endless sittings.

15.2 Exercise 2

Instructions for exercise

1 Key in the text below, pressing RETURN twice at the end of each line and save it as EX15C.

2 Print out one copy (Section 3.1) before formatting.

3 Put the whole notice into double line spacing (Section 5.3) so that it is well spaced out.

4 Set the margins at 1 inch (Section 5.6).

5 Embolden GRAND JUMBLE SALE (Section 8.2).

6 Underline the headings starting Saturday ... and at St Matthews ... (Section 8.1).

7 Embolden IN AID OF SCHOOL FUNDS (Section 8.2).

8 Italicise ALL ARE WELCOME (Section 8.3).

9 Centre all the text (Section 5.2).

10 Centre the page (Section 7.7).

11 Print out a final copy after the formatting has been completed (Section 3.1) and save the document as EX15D.

```
GRAND JUMBLE SALE

to be held on

Saturday, -- March 199-

at St Matthews School, Harpenden

at 2.30 pm

IN AID OF SCHOOL FUNDS

ALL ARE WELCOME
```

Your document should look like the example below when you have
finished following the instructions.

GRAND JUMBLE SALE

to be held on

<u>Saturday, -- March 199-</u>

<u>at St Matthews School, Harpenden</u>

at 2.30 pm

IN AID OF SCHOOL FUNDS

ALL ARE WELCOME

15.3 Exercise 3

Instructions for exercise

1 Key in the agenda below and save it as EX15E. Print it out without
formatting.

2 Use the block marking facility (Section 6.1) to select text for formatting.

3 Centre the headings (Section 5.2) and embolden them (Section 8.2).

4 Use the feature of typing in the left margin for numbering the agenda
(Section 7.6) and use the paragraph numbering feature (Section 10.4).

5 Use inset paragraphs for sub-paragraphs, numbered (a) and (b) (Section 7.5).

6 Put the inset paragraphs in italics (Section 8.3).

7 Save the exercise again as EX15F and print out a revised copy.

AGENDA

Annual General Meeting

of Sports and Social Club

to be held on Wednesday, 9th January, 1991

at 10 am in Committee Room A

1   Apologies for Absence

2   Minutes of Last Annual General Meeting

3   Chairman's Report

4   Officers' Reports:

        (a)   Treasurer's Report
        (b)   Secretary's Report

5   Report on Christmas Party

6   Works' Outing at Easter

7   Repairs to Club House

        (a)   Progress to Date
        (b)   Future Developments

8   Any Other Business

9   Date of Next Meeting

Your completed agenda should look like the example given below.

AGENDA

Annual General Meeting

of Sports and Social Club

to be held on Wednesday, 9th January, 1991

at 10 am in Committee Room A

1   Apologies for Absence

2   Minutes of Last Annual General Meeting

3   Chairman's Report

4   Officers' Reports:

        (a)   *Treasurer's Report*
        (b)   *Secretary's Report*

5   Report on Christmas Party

6   Works' Outing at Easter

7   Repairs to Club House

        (a)   *Progress to Date*
        (b)   *Future Developments*

8   Any Other Business

9   Date of Next Meeting

15.4   Exercise 4

Instructions for exercise

1 Key in the exercise below and save it as EX15G. It is suggested that you do all the formatting as you key it in. So you will need to read the following instructions before commencing the exercise.

2 Set the left margin at 1.5 inches and the right margin at 1 inch (Section 5.6).

3 Centre (Section 5.2) and embolden the main headings (Section 8.2).

4 Use the typing in the left margin feature for putting the numbers into the left margin (Section 7.6) and use the paragraph numbering feature (Section 10.11) to number the minutes.

5 Underline the side headings (Section 8.1).

6 Use the forced page break facility to set sensible page breaks (Section 10.2), so that they do not occur in the middle of a short numbered paragraph.

7 Use the page numbering facility (Section 10.4) to number the pages of the minutes.

8 Give these minutes a header of *AGM/91* (Section 10.5), using italics for the header text (Section 8.3).

9 Use the hyphenation control (Section 10.9).

10 Justify the document (Section 5.4).

11 Use the View Printing facility (Section 5.5) to see how the document will look.

12 Print out a copy of the document.

Minutes of Annual General Meeting

of Sports and Social Club

held on Wednesday, 9th January, 1991

at 10 am in Committee Room A

Present:

Margaret Harris	Chairman
Peter Goldstein	Treasurer
Marie Jacquard	Secretary
Rajesh Patel	Sub-committee (Christmas Party)
Dave Williams	Sub-committee (Christmas Party)
Nelum Wijayapala	Sub-committee (Christmas Party)

Marilyn Stephens   Working Party Club House
Neville Hartley   Working Party Club House
plus 60 ordinary members

1   Apologies for Absence

Apologies were received from Nader Moghaddam and Edward
Tomalin.

2   Minutes of Last Annual General Meeting

These were agreed to be a correct record.

3   Chairman's Report

The Chairman reported that membership had increased by
10% during 1990 and that there were now 196 members of
the Sports and Social Club.

4   Officers' Reports:

(a)   Treasurer's Report

         The Treasurer reported that funds were healthy
         and that the club had £256 in their building
         society account. A copy of the Report and
         Accounts were circulated to all members at the
         meeting and this is attached to these minutes.

(b)   Secretary's Report

         The Secretary reported that a number of
         successful Social events had been held during
         the year which had been well supported by
         members.

5   <u>Report on Christmas Party</u>

The Christmas Party was well attended - by 80% of the
members - and it was agreed that an enjoyable time had
been had by all. A special vote of thanks was given to
the catering sub-committee who had organised this event.
After some general discussion, it was agreed to continue
the tradition of the Christmas party.

6   <u>Works' Outing at Easter</u>

Suggestions were invited from members for a suitable
Works outing at Easter. A boat trip to Windsor was one
suggestion, another suggestion was a theatre trip to the
West End, and a third suggestion was a trip to Alton
Towers.

It was agreed members would forward suggestions to the
committee and a draft document would be circulated for
members to choose the outing they would like. A decision
would be based on the wishes of the majority of the
members.

7   <u>Repairs to Club House</u>

(a)   *Progress to Date*

The roof repairs after the recent storm are now
virtually complete. The contractor has reported
that the work would be 100% complete by the end of
January.

(b)   *Future Developments*

It was agreed that estimates should be obtained for
repainting the exterior of the club house. These
estimates will be dealt with by a separate sub-
committee of the club house working party.

8   <u>Any Other Business</u>

There was no other business.

9   <u>Date of Next Meeting</u>

The date of the next Annual General Meeting was set for
Wednesday, 8th January 1992.

15.5 Exercise 5

In this exercise you key in a standard letter (which is from a Hospital Secretary to patients asking them to come to see the specialist) and merge it with three names and addresses given below to form a personalised letter, to practise the mail merge feature of WordPerfect. You may care to add names and addresses of your own to the list that is given.

The mail merge feature is detailed in Chapter 12.

Instructions for exercise

1 Key in the following letter and save it as EX15H.

2 Remember to press CTRL and F before each field name.

    ^Ftodaysdate^F

    ^Ftitle^F ^Finitials^F ^Fsurname^F
    ^Faddress^F

    Dear ^Ftitle^F ^Fsurname^F

    An appointment has been made for you at ^Ftime^F on
    ^Fdate^F to see ^Fspecialist^F.
    Please report to ^Fward^F promptly.

Yours sincerely

Hospital Secretary

3 Key in the data for your secondary file and save it as EX15J.

4 You will need to list your fieldnames at the start of your secondary file, as shown in Chapter 12. A quick reminder, hold CTRL and type 'N', press RETURN at the end of first line. Key in the fieldnames, emboldening them as you key them in, starting a new line with each fieldname. Hold CTRL and type 'R', hold CTRL and key in 'E' to denote end of fieldnames, hold CTRL and press RETURN to put the fieldnames on a separate page from the records which will follow.

5 Key in the information to complete the data for each record. Do not forget to hold CTRL and press R at the end of each section of information entered under each fieldname, pressing CTRL and E at the end of each record and CTRL and RETURN to denote the start of a new record.

Your exercise should be keyed in as follows:

^N
title
initials
surname
address
todaysdate
date
specialist
ward
^R
^E
CTRL and RETURN

Mr^R

```
N^R
Moghaddam^R
66 Berkeley Close
LIVERPOOL^R
20th January 1991^R
31st January 1991^R
Mr Mohdbadia^R
Rosemary^R
^E
CTRL and RETURN
Mrs^R
D^R
Van Horn^R
Flat 6
Alpine Mansions
Castle Street
NORWICH^R
20th January 1991^R
16th February 1991^R
Mr Solomons^R
Iris^R
^E
CTRL and RETURN
Miss^R
F^R
Aitlkboud^R
22 St Davids Road
EXETER^R
20th January 1991^R
16th February 1991^R
Mrs Macpherson^R
Daisy^R
^E
CTRL and RETURN
```

6 Now merge the two exercises to form the personalised letter, and save this, if you wish, as EX15K.

7 Print out a copy of each personal letter.

15.6 Exercise 6

Instructions for exercise

1 Key in the text below and save it as EX15L.

2 Set the margins at 1.5 inches (Section 5.6).

3 Set left-aligned tab stops for columns 2 - 4 (Section 7.1) at 2, 3.5 and 5 inches.

4 Print out a copy of the table at this stage.

5 Change the margins to 1 inch to give wider spacing between the columns (Section 5.6).

6 Move the tab stops to 1.5, 3 and 4.5 inches.

7 Use sorting facility on column 2 to put the shrubs into alphabetical order (Section 14.3).

8 Draw a box around the table (Section 14.5).

9 Print out the revised table and save it as EX15M.

Key	Shrub	Location	Season
1	Erica	sunny	all year
2	Magnolia	sunny	Spring
3	Rhododendron	sunny/shade	Spring/Summer
4	Berberis	sunny	all year
5	Viburnum	sunny	Summer
6	Juniper	sunny/shade	all year
7	Pieris	sunny/shade	Spring
8	Broom	sunny	Summer

9	Skimmia	sunny/shade	all year
10	Pyracantha	sunny/shade	Autumn

Your sorted table should look like the example below.

Key	Shrub	Location	Season
4	Berberis	sunny	all year
8	Broom	sunny	Summer
1	Erica	sunny	all year
6	Juniper	sunny/shade	all year
2	Magnolia	sunny	Spring
7	Pieris	sunny/shade	Spring
10	Pyracantha	sunny/shade	Autumn
3	Rhododendron	sunny/shade	Spring/Summer
9	Skimmia	sunny/shade	all year
5	Viburnum	sunny	Summer

16 INSTALLING WORDPERFECT

16.1 Before you begin the installation procedure ____

When you buy a software package like WordPerfect it has to be **installed** on your particular computer before it will run properly. Installing means copying the program from the floppy disks onto the computer in such a way that the computer will be able to operate the software.

You should always take a copy of the original (or **master**) disks and work from the copies, keeping the masters safe. The reason for this is that even if your program is **corrupted** (damaged, destroyed or inadvertently altered), you will still have the original version which you could re-copy. This will mean either copying them onto the hard disk or onto floppy disks.

Furthermore, although WordPerfect contains instructions, within its program, to enable text to be displayed on the screen, printed out on paper or stored on disk, it needs to know in advance what sort of screen, printer, disk drives etc. are going to be used.

The first thing you need to ascertain, therefore, is the type of equipment you have. The WordPerfect manual gives you a list of the information you need to know. You may have to check in your computer's manual to do this. The following, however, are some questions which you will need to be able to answer:

- Does your computer have a hard disk drive, or two floppy disk drives?
- Does it have a colour or monochrome screen?
- What type of printer will you be using, and is it parallel or serial?

It is particularly important that you familiarise yourself with the specification of your printer if you want to realise the package's full potential in terms of formatting and displaying printed text. Your printer will probably have a separate manual of its own where all the relevant information will be given.

Before you begin the installation procedure you should have all the floppy disks containing the WordPerfect program, the WordPerfect manual and the manuals for your computer and printer to hand.

If you are using a twin floppy disk machine, you will need a copy of the DOS disk as well. If you have a hard disk, a version of DOS will be held there.

From now on the instructions for installation will depend on whether you are going to use hard or floppy disks for storing the program.

16.2 Installation procedure for hard disk systems ___

The first step is to turn on your computer. If you are prompted to fill in the date and the time, do so and C> should be displayed on your screen. If it is not, key-in 'cd c:' and press ENTER.

Now you need to find out whether your version of DOS (stored on the hard disk) contains a small, but vital file. This file is called **config.sys**. To do this you key in 'type config.sys' and press ENTER. Your screen will now either tell you that this file does not exist or it will list the contents of the file. If the latter, check that it contains the information files=20 (or more) and buffers=5 (or more). If the former, you will need to create this file.

You do this by keying-in 'copy config.sys+con config.sys' and press ENTER. Your screen will display the word CON. Now press ENTER again and key-in 'files=20' and press ENTER, then 'buffers=5' and press ENTER. Now hold down CTRL and press 'z', then press ENTER again. Your screen will display ^z. You have created the config.sys file. Turn off your computer and then turn it on again.

Before you copy the WordPerfect program onto your hard disk it is a good idea to create a **directory** (a named storage area) on your disk specifically for WordPerfect files only. To do this you key in 'md wp50' (or 'md wp51' for WordPerfect version 5.1) and press ENTER. The directory has been created. Now key in 'cd wp50' to go into this new directory and the screen will display C:\WP50.

Now everything is ready to start actually copying the program from its original floppy disks onto your hard disk. Place the floppy disk labelled WordPerfect 1 into your floppy disk drive and key in 'copy a:*.*' and press ENTER. On your screen you will see the names of the files displayed as they are being copied. When the screen displays C:\WP50 again you will know the copying process is complete for that floppy disk.

Follow this same procedure with the WordPerfect 2 floppy disk, then the Speller and Thesaurus floppy disks.

All of them should now be safely installed on your hard disk.

Place the floppy disk labelled Fonts/Graphics in your floppy disk drive and key-in 'copy a:*.frs' and press ENTER. When the screen display C:\WP50 reappears you can continue by keying-in 'copy a:*.drs' and press ENTER. These files contain instructions about printing which are needed if you want your printed output from WordPerfect to display all your text formatting commands (i.e. italics, bold, justifying etc).

The WordPerfect program is ready to run on your computer now and all you need to do is to key-in 'wp' and press ENTER at the C:\WP50 screen prompt. Enter your 11-digit licence number at the prompt and you will be into the package.

The first time you load WordPerfect you will be asked to select the printer(s) you will be using. The procedure for doing this is the same for both floppy and hard disk systems and the instructions are given in 16.4.

16.3 Installation procedure for twin floppy disk systems

The reason for taking copies of the master disks of WordPerfect onto floppy disks is to provide you with back-up copies from which you will always work, rather than risk damaging the originals.

You will need to have the same number of blank floppy disks ready as there are WordPerfect disks in your pack. (You may not wish, however, to copy the Learning disk if you are not going to use it.) You will also need a floppy disk containing MSDOS.

The number of disks you will need depends on whether your computer uses 5.25 or 3.5 inch disks. If the former you will have a WordPerfect 1 disk and a WordPerfect 2 disk, but on the smaller-sized disks you will only need one disk: WordPerfect 1/WordPerfect 2, because the smaller disks have a higher storage capacity.

Before you can use your blank floppy disks they must be **formatted** (prepared for their storage function). To do this place your DOS disk in drive A and switch on the computer. The screen will display A>. Key in 'format b:' and press ENTER. You will be prompted to place your new disk in drive B and press any key to continue. The screen will tell you when this procedure is complete (you may first be prompted for LABEL, just press RETURN) and ask you if you wish to format another disk. Respond to this prompt by keying in 'Y' and placing the next blank disk in drive B. Follow this procedure, responding appropriately to the screen prompts until you have formatted all the required blank floppy disks. Label them up in the same way as the master disks are labelled, using a felt tip pen. (If you write with a hard-tipped pen such as a biro, it can damage the disk.)

At this stage you will need to find out whether your version of DOS (stored on the MSDOS floppy disk) contains a small, but vital file. This file is called **config.sys**. To do this you key-in 'type a:config.sys' and press ENTER. Your screen will now either tell you that this file does not exist or it will list the contents of the file. If the latter, check that it contains the information files=20 (or more) and buffers=5 (or more). If the former, you will need to create this file.

You do this by keying-in 'copy a:config.sys+con a:config.sys' and press ENTER. Your screen will display the word CON. Now press ENTER again and key-in 'files=20' and press ENTER, then 'buffers=5' and press ENTER. Now hold down CTRL and press 'z', then press ENTER again. Your screen will display ^z. You have created the config.sys file. Turn off your computer and then turn it on again.

Always use this particular MSDOS floppy disk to start up your system.

You could actually copy the DOS files onto your copy of the back-up floppy disk WordPerfect 1, but it is not recommended if you are using 5.25 inch floppy disks as their storage capacity is limited.

You are now ready to copy the WordPerfect program from its original disks onto your formatted, pre-labelled blank floppy disks.

Place the WordPerfect 1 disk into the A (left hand) drive of your computer and with the A> prompt displayed on your screen, key-in 'copy a:*.* b:' and press ENTER. You will notice the filenames on this disk displayed on the screen as they are copied across. When the A> prompt reappears, the procedure is complete. Repeat this procedure for the remaining master disks, always remembering to place the originals in drive A and the formatted blank disks in drive B.

Store the master disks somewhere secure in case you need to take more back-up copies at a future date.

You are now ready to load and run WordPerfect.

Place the MSDOS disk (containing the config.sys file as described above) in drive A and turn-on your computer. When the A> prompt appears, remove the MSDOS disk and replace it with the back-up version of WordPerfect 1 and at the same time place a Printer disk in drive B.

Key in 'b:' and press ENTER and the B> prompt will be displayed. Then proceed to key in 'a:wp' to start running WordPerfect. Replace the WordPerfect 1 disk in drive A with the WordPerfect 2 disk (not necessary if your are using the smaller-sized disks which hold all the files on one disk).

The first time you use WordPerfect it will need to know what sort of printer you are going to be using. The procedure for doing this is given below.

16.4 Selecting printers

This procedure is virtually the same whether you have a hard or twin floppy disk system. It is something you *only* do the first time you load and run your WordPerfect program.

You load the WordPerfect program using the appropriate procedure as described above.

Hold down the SHIFT key while you press F7 and the Print menu will be displayed. Key in 's' to access the Select Printer menu and then select '2' to display a list of printers available for printing WordPerfect.

(If you are using a twin floppy disk system and the printer you wish to use is not on the list you must select '2' and insert an alternative Printer disk.)

Move the cursor down to highlight the name of the printer you wish to choose and press ENTER.

A message Updating Font appears on the screen and, when this has cleared, press F7 to exit and go into the Select Printer: Edit menu. The settings displayed on the screen will probably not need changing, but if they do, select the appropriate number and follow the instructions for changing the setting. (Refer to your printer manual for information.) When you are happy with the settings, key in the name of the printer driver (see above) and press ENTER. Now press F7 to exit the Printer Settings menu and return to the Select Printer menu. Your printer driver name should be displayed on this screen; press F7 again and you are now ready to commence your first word processing task in WordPerfect.

USE OF FUNCTION KEYS AND QUICK CURSOR MOVEMENT SUMMARY

In your WordPerfect manual you will find a template which is placed around the keyboard to give guidance about the use of the function keys. Should this be mislaid or accidentally destroyed, here is a quick reference for you to keep at hand when using the package.

You will find the function keys located either to the left of or above your standard keyboard. To provide more than one function per key WordPerfect uses each "F" key in conjunction with three further keys (as well as being used alone). These keys are: **CTRL** (control), **SHIFT**, **ALT** (alternative). Locate these three keys on your own keyboard before going any further – we cannot give you the precise location as keyboards differ.

Key	Alone	+ALT	+CTRL	+SHIFT
F1	Cancel	Thesaurus	Shell	Setup
F2	Search	Replace	Spell	Search
F3	Help	Reveal Codes	Screen	Switch
F4	Indent	Block	Move	Indent
F5	List Files	Mark Text	Text In/Out	Date/Outline
F6	Bold	Flush Right	Tab Align	Centre
F7	Exit	Math/Column	Footnote	Print
F8	Underline	Style	Font	Format
F9	Merge R	Graphics	Merge/Sort	Merge Codes
F10	Save	Macro	Macro Del	Retrieve
F11	Reveal Codes*			
F12	Block*			

* Some computers have these two extra function keys on their keyboard and you can see from the above table how they can be used as an alternative to ALT F3 and ALT F4.

Another quick reference which you may find useful to have at hand while working is the following list of rapid cursor movements.

Shortcut	*Keys to press*
End of Line	Press END key.
Start of Line	Press HOME key and then left cursor key.
Move one word left or right	Hold CTRL and press left or right cursor key.
Move to start of file	Press HOME key twice and press upward cursor key.
Move to end of file	Press HOME key twice and press downward cursor key.
Move to top of page	Press PGUP key.
Move to bottom of page	Press PGDOWN key.
Move to top of screen	Press HOME key and up cursor key or − (minus) key
Move to bottom of screen	Press HOME key and down cursor key or + (plus) key

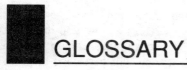

GLOSSARY

Term	Explanation
backup file	This is a file which is automatically created by the word processor when a document is saved for a second or subsequent time and is the last but one version of a document. In other words, if you have saved a document three times, the first version will have been lost, if you have used the same filename each time. It will have the file extension 'BK!' on your directory of files.
block	Text must be blocked or marked by WordPerfect before it is moved, deleted, copied, or formatted in some way, such as put into italics. WordPerfect requires you to mark the beginning and end of the text you wish to alter in some way.
buffer	A temporary memory used for storing text or instructions until processing takes place. There is a buffer memory for text which has been keyed in which stores text until it has been processed by the CPU and also the print buffer which stores text to be printed.
byte	A unit of storage, equal to one character. A computer with 1 Mb (Megabyte) of RAM memory is capable of storing more than 1 million characters.
character	Any single item of text keyed in such as letters, numbers, commas, etc.
corruption	The accidental destruction of text on a disk, possibly caused by mishandling of the disk.
CPU	Central Processing Unit, the 'brain' of the computer.

cursor   This is a line which appears underneath a character or space on the computer screen to show you the exact place where you are in a document. If you wish to insert or delete any text, you will first need to place your cursor at the required position in the document.

decimal tab   The alignment of a column of figures at the decimal point.

cut and paste   The process of moving text or graphics from one part of a document to another.

default   A format setting or value already given by the program for carrying out a specific task e.g. WordPerfect comes with a default setting of a ragged right margin, which can be altered by the operator if necessary.

directory   This is a list of files. Your disks can be divided into separate directories to keep your files separate and in some sort of order, as one would keep files in a separate drawer of a filing cabinet.

dot matrix   An impact printer commonly used, whereby printing is done by the action of groups of pins striking against a fabric or carbon ribbon, forming characters on the paper copy. Generally, two qualities of print are available with this sort of printer, NLQ (Near Letter Quality) and draft. The former is used for print outs where the quality is of paramount importance. Draft quality is used where you know the text is likely to be altered, and you require a copy for proof reading and alteration purposes only.

DOS   Disk Operating System. A computer program which co-ordinates the overall running of a computer. It also enables the computer to 'understand' application programs, such as WordPerfect word processing, so that they can take place. MSDOS is the disk operating system produced by Microsoft.

edit   Any alterations made to the text.

embolden	To make characters stand out from the page by making them darker than the rest of the text. They are printed twice by a dot matrix printer.
file	A copy of a document saved on a floppy or hard disk.
floppy disk	A disk of plastic with a magnetic coating which will store the equivalent of a paperback book. The capacity of disks can vary according to their density.
format (text)	The display or appearance of text, e.g. margins, line spacing, italics, bold, etc.
format (disk)	Preparing a new floppy disk ready for use on a particular computer system and making it possible for the computer to store information on it and retrieve it for editing.
function keys	Keys found on a computer keyboard labelled (usually) F1 - F10, which can be used either alone or in combination with other keys to carry out operations. WordPerfect's word processing program is very reliant on these keys to access the various menus.
hard disk	A disk or series of disks made of metal coated with magnetic oxide, which can store large amounts of data and operates more quickly than a floppy disk. It gives permanent storage of computer programs and working files when the computer is switched off.
hardware	All computer equipment which is tangible, such as the keyboard, screen, etc. as opposed to software which is information or instructions for the computer.
justify	A straight right margin of text so that it appears like the left margin of text.
K (or Kb)	Kilobyte. A unit of main memory or disk storage capacity, approximately 1000 bytes.
laser printer	A non-impact printer, which uses a laser beam to form the characters. Used to give a high quality appearance to printed work.

lower case   Text in small letters.

macro   A single command that will enable the computer to carry out several instructions.

mail merge   The word processing term for combining a standard letter with a list of names and addresses to produce a seemingly personalised letter. The word processing program carries out the procedure automatically.

M (or Mb)   Megabyte. A unit of disk or main memory storage capacity, approximately 1 million bytes or characters.

MSDOS   This stands for Microsoft Disk Operating System. It may be loaded into a computer's memory before a computer program, such as WordPerfect, can be used by the computer. See 'DOS'.

NLQ   Near Letter Quality. The highest quality output from a dot-matrix printer.

orphan   The last line of a paragraph that appears by itself at the top of a page.

page break   The point at which the page will break before a new page is started. Page breaks will occur automatically with WordPerfect, but the operator can override this and introduce page breaks where required.

password   A special word to prevent access to either a computer file or the computer itself, i.e. a security device.

peripherals   Any of the computer hardware other than the central processing unit (CPU).

RAM   Random Access Memory. Part of the computer's memory in the CPU used to store programs and data. The contents of the RAM are lost when the computer is switched off.

re-formatting Altering the appearance of the text on page, by changing the margins, line spacing, justification, etc.

repagination   A word processing facility that allows text in a long document to be moved automatically to new pages, when new text is inserted or existing text deleted.

ruler An on-screen guide showing the positions of tab stops in WordPerfect.

save To store text or data permanently on either the hard disk or a floppy disk.

screen dump The screen display produced as a printed output.

scrolling Quick cursor movement through the text displayed on screen, towards the top or bottom of the document.

software Programmed instructions written for the computer to control the hardware.

status line A line at the bottom of the screen in WordPerfect giving information about the current document, the current page you are working on, and the position of the cursor on screen.

subscript A subscript character is one that is partially below the line, e.g. H_2O.

superscript A superscript character is one that is partially above the line, e.g. $100°F$.

toggle key A key which, pressed once, will activate a particular function, and, pressed again, will switch it off, e.g. CAPS LOCK.

uppercase Text in capital letters.

variable An item of information in a standard document that will vary, e.g. name, date, etc. Variables can be stored in a data file and automatically inserted into a standard document.

widow The first line of a paragraph that is left by itself at the foot of a page.

wordwrap A process whereby a word is automatically taken from the end of one line to the start of the next if it is too long to fit.

OTHER TITLES AVAILABLE
IN TEACH YOURSELF

☐	0 340 54921 1	**Choosing the Right Computer**	£5.99
☐	0 340 53904 6	**dBase III PLUS – book**	£5.99
☐	0 340 55795 8	**dBase III PLUS –**	
		book/disk pack	£14.99
☐	0 340 55868 7	**Desktop Publishing**	£5.99
☐	0 340 55431 2	**Lotus 123 – book**	£5.99
☐	0 340 53906 2	**Lotus 123 – book/disk pack**	£14.99
☐	0 340 53905 4	**WordStar 6 – book**	£5.99
☐	0 340 55428 2	**WordStar 6 – book/disk pack**	£14.99

All these books are available at your local bookshop or newsagent, or can be ordered direct from the publisher. Just tick the titles you want and fill in the form below.

Prices and availability subject to change without notice.

HODDER & STOUGHTON PAPERBACKS, PO Box 11, Falmouth, Cornwall.

Please send cheque or postal order for the value of the book, and add the following for postage and packing:

UK including BFPO – £1.00 for one book, plus 50p for the second book, and 30p for each additional book ordered up to a £3.00 maximum.

OVERSEAS INCLUDING EIRE – £2.00 for the first book, plus £1.00 for the second book, and 50p for each additional book ordered.
OR please debit this amount from my Access/Visa card (delete as appropriate).

Card number ☐☐☐☐☐☐☐☐☐☐☐☐☐☐☐☐

AMOUNT £..

EXPIRY DATE ....

SIGNED ....

NAME..

ADDRESS...